LEADERSHIP YOU CAN HAVE WHAT IT TAKES

Charles Nieman

WORD OF FAITH
LEADERSHIP AND BIBLE INSTITUTE

**All Scripture quotations
from the King James Version
of the Bible unless otherwise stated**

ISBN 0-914307-08-8

Printed in the United States of America
Copyright © 1983 **WORD OF FAITH PUBLISHING**
PO Box 819000, Dallas, Texas 75381
All Rights Reserved

TABLE OF CONTENTS

INTRODUCTION

Chapter I
COURAGE — 1

Chapter II
THE ORIGINS OF FEAR — 21

Chapter III
THE FRUITS OF FEAR — 51

Chapter IV
HOW TO OVERCOME FEAR WHEN YOU REALIZE IT IS PRESENT WITH YOU — 57

Chapter V
BECOMING A FEARLESS LEADER — 73

Chapter VI
THE NON-COMPROMISING LEADER — 89

Chapter VII
YOU CAN BE A LEADER — 105

Chapter VIII
DRESSED FIT TO RUN — 111

Chapter IX
THE DECISION IS YOURS 121

Chapter X
FAITHFULNESS AND INTEGRITY 127

Chapter XI
WOMEN, LEADERS, AND THE BIBLE 149

Chapter XII
SEEDS OF LEADERSHIP 181

INTRODUCTION

Have you ever wondered what makes some people leaders? I have asked myself that question for many years.

What is it that makes people into leaders? Is it merely chance, or can you do things that will cause you to become a leader? These are questions I have asked myself many times.

As a pastor of a large, growing church, I am expected to lead and required to lead my congregation. The people in my church expect me to be a leader. If I am going to fulfill God's call upon my life, I am required to be a leader.

In order to accomplish the vision God has given me for my life, I have purposed to observe the lives of leaders. I have purposed to see what it is they have that makes them leaders.

In doing this I have discovered common traits in all of the leaders I have observed. I will talk about those traits in this book.

Webster's Dictionary defines leadership as simply having the ability to lead. It defines a leader as someone who leads or conducts; a guide; a conductor; a chief; a commander; a captain; one who goes first. A leader is someone whose life is an example to other people.

Leadership: You Can Have What It Takes

Throughout history there have always been leaders—men and women who were at the front of the line, leading people in the right paths to take. There have been people who have stood up to adversity and tyranny, and those who blazed new trails.

At this time, in the course of the human race, a cry has gone out for men and women who will step forward and be in the front. I believe those people will be members of the body of Christ.

This is the greatest hour the body of Christ has ever had to fulfill its destiny as the light of the world and the salt of the earth, as in Matthew 5:13-15. I believe God wants the church to come to the forefront in the world on a collective basis, and on an individual basis.

The church is comprised of individuals. We are each members of His body. We have important roles to play in the development of the body of Christ and the advancement of God's kingdom in the earth.

Before an army can advance, it must have leaders. Those leaders must believe in what they are doing. All Christians believe in the advancement of Christianity. We are commissioned to make that a priority in our lives (Matthew 6:33).

The Kingdom of God is advanced on all levels, not just from the church in its weekly services. It is advanced on our jobs, in our neighborhoods, and in the political arena.

In each area of life, God desires for His people to be leaders. This is clearly revealed to us .

13 Christ has redeemed us from the curse of the law, being made a curse for us: for it is written, Cursed is every one that hangeth on a tree:

14 That the blessing of Abraham might come on the Gentiles through Jesus Christ; that we might receive the promise of the Spirit through faith. (Galatians 3:13-14)

1 And it shall come to pass, if thou shalt hearken diligently unto the voice of the LORD thy God, to observe and to do all his commandments which I command thee this day, that the Lord thy God will set thee on high above all nations of the earth:

2 And all these blessings shall come on thee, and overtake thee, if thou shalt hearken unto the voice of the LORD thy God.

3 Blessed shalt thou be in the city, and blessed shalt thou be in the field.

4 Blessed shall be the fruit of thy body, and the fruit of thy ground, and the fruit of thy cattle, the increase of thy kine, and the flocks of thy sheep.

5 Blessed shall be thy basket and thy store.

6 Blessed shalt thou be when thou comest in, and blessed shalt thou be when thou goest out.

7 The LORD shall cause thine enemies that rise up against thee to be smitten before thy face: they shall come out against thee one way, and flee before thee seven ways.

8 The LORD shall command the blessing upon thee in thy storehouses, and in all that thou set-

test thine hand unto; and he shall bless thee in the land which the LORD thy God giveth thee.

10 And all people of the earth shall see that thou art called by the name of the LORD; and they shall be afraid of thee.

11 And the LORD shall make thee plenteous in goods, in the fruit of thy body, and in the fruit of thy cattle, and in the fruit of thy ground, in the land which the LORD sware unto thy fathers to give thee.

12 The LORD shall open unto thee his good treasure, the heaven to give the rain unto thy land in his season, and to bless all the work of thine hand: and thou shalt lend unto many nations, and thou shalt not borrow.

13 And the LORD shall make thee the head, and not the tail; and thou shalt be above only, and thou shalt not be beneath; if that thou hearken unto the commandments of the LORD thy God, which I command thee this day, to observe and to do them:

14 And thou shalt not go aside from any of the words which I command thee this day, to the right hand, or to the left, to go after other gods to serve them. (Deuteronomy 28:1-14)

Through the substitutionary sacrifice of Jesus, the blessings of Abraham have come upon you and me. Part of those blessings is that **we are to be the head and not the tail, above only, and not beneath! God wants us to be leaders!**

Introduction

This book draws its information on leadership from the Bible.

Why?

The Bible contains the history of some of the world's greatest leaders. In its pages are detailed accounts of their lives and the revelation of how God used them to accomplish great things to change the course of destiny.

By studying the lives of such people as Joseph, Moses, Joshua, David, Esther, Solomon, Jesus, and Paul, I have discovered that people look for certain qualities in their leaders. I will discuss those qualities and show how every believer can have what it takes to be a leader.

What do people look for in a leader? Before I tell you, remember—you can only lead when people will follow. People want their leaders to have wisdom, courage, strength, God's anointing in their life, a vision, and dedication.

People expect leaders to be faithful and have integrity. A leader's life must be an example to those who follow them. They must live lives without compromise, and be fearless.

Throughout this book, these qualities are covered in such a way that, as you read them, you will learn how to develop them in your life through the power of God's Word.

Remember—what the Lord has done for one, He will do for all. God wants for you to be the head and not the tail, above only, and not beneath. In summary, God wants each of us to be winners in life and He has made provision in His Word so **we can have what it takes!**

Chapter 1

COURAGE

When the Lord first called my wife and me into the ministry I was a spiritual illiterate. I didn't know one book of the Bible from another. When a speaker would tell us to turn to the book of Ephesians, I would turn to the Table of Contents.

While I was going through the Table of Contents, trying to find the book of Ephesians, they would go to Thessalonians, and I would be back at the Table of Contents.

By the time I got to Thessalonians they had been to Daniel and Isaiah and all the way back to Corinthians At this point I would give up. I would close my Bible and buy the tapes. Then as I listened to them, I would push the pause button, and the speaker would wait for me. I was a spiritual illiterate.

I had been saved for four or five years. Like many people in the Body of Christ, I lived a defeated life. I loved

Jesus, but I had no power until I was filled with the Holy Ghost. Then my life changed like the change from night to day.

You cannot live the victorious Christian life without power. Walking by faith is not for sissies.

I used to think Christians were a bunch of losers. I thought they were people trying to take the easy way out.

I am telling you that living by faith is not the easy way out. Living by faith will be one of the toughest things you will ever do, but the rewards are worth it. There is nothing like victory. There is absolutely nothing that can compare with victory. You were made to walk in victory. Get that thought into your mind and into your heart. **You were made for victory**

You were made in the image and likeness of God. God is victorious. God is not a loser. He does not plan to lose. He does not make provision to lose. God is a winner, and you were made in the image and likeness of God--so that makes you a winner!

It is in your heart to be a winner. You were not made to be a good loser. I'm not saying you should be a bad sport. You are supposed to be a good sport. But you are not made to be a good loser.

...this is the victory that overcometh the world, even our faith. (1st John 5:4)

God has called us to walk in victory.

After we had been in the ministry for a year, the Lord opened a door for us to move to Fort Worth, Texas and work for Jerry Savelle and Kenneth Copeland, aiding them in their teaching seminars.

Courage

When we moved, the total weight of our furniture was four hundred pounds. We had an old broken down naugahide chair, a big zebra-skin pillow, a color TV, and a "no matter where you started out sleeping you ended up in the middle" roll-away bed.

I was under the impression that when we moved to Fort Worth and found a house, a man would drive up to me and say, "I don't know what this is all about, but an angel appeared to me and told me to bring you this furniture."

Needless to say, that didn't happen.

Here we were, Rochelle and I, working with Kenneth Copeland and Jerry Savelle. We were traveling all over the United States. I was in every service that these men taught on faith. I was in church more than anyone else. And when I went home, I had to sit on the floor. We sat on the floor for nine months. I would get excited when I had to go out of town, because then I could stay in a motel room and sit on real furniture.

We knew all the right things to do. You couldn't get us to make a bad confession. You couldn't get us to say things out of our mouths that were wrong. But the Word was not working in our lives the way it should.

I could not understand why. I listened to what Brother Copeland said, and I went home and did what I thought he said to do. Then I would watch him get blessed, and I would sit on the floor. That can be frustrating; that can be discouraging.

After six months, the Lord began to finally break through our darkness. He taught us three basic revelations that changed our lives. It took about three months for these revelations to fit together and produce. Finally, after nine months, we got up off of the floor, because we were able to buy some furniture.

The first thing God taught us was what it meant to be in Christ. We discovered we are as much in Christ as Christ is in the Father (John 17:23) That truth set us free.

The second thing we discovered was how to use our confession as a weapon. We discovered it from Charles Capps. We were very careful to say the right things at the right time in our daily conversation.

We had never before seen the fact that we needed to purposely, on a regular disciplined basis, say about our lives what God has said about them. We began to do that, and the chains which had been holding us began to break off of us.

The third thing He began to teach us was about fear; if fear is in your heart, your faith well not work. The Word will not produce on your behalf the way it should, if there is fear in your heart.

Fear is a spiritual force. It does not come out of your head. It comes out of your heart.

Faith is the force of the kingdom of God. It will go forth into the kingdom of God to lay hold upon the things you desire. It will bring them to you and make them a reality in yor life.

Fear is the power force of the kingdom of darkness. It will go forth into that kingdom to lay hold upon the things you are afraid of, making them a reality in your life. Fear will lay hold upon the things you are afraid of. It will bring them to you and make them a reality in your life.

For the thing which I greatly feared is come upon me, and that which I was afraid of is come upon me. (Job 3:25)

Actually, fear is faith going in the wrong direction. With that in mind, I want to look at Joshua--one of the greatest leaders in the Bible.

1 Now after the death of Moses the servant of the LORD it came to pass, that the LORD spake unto Joshua the son of Nun, Moses' minister, saying,

2 Moses my servant is dead; now therefore arise, go over this Jordan, thou, and all this people, unto the land which I do give to them, even to the children of Israel.

3 Every place that the sole of your foot shall tread upon, that have I given unto you, as I said unto Moses.

4 From the wilderness and this Lebanon even unto the great river, the river Euphrates, all the land of the Hittites, and unto the great sea toward the going down to the sun, shall be your coast.

5 There shall not any man be able to stand before thee all the days of thy life: as I was with Moses, so I will be with thee: I will not fail thee, nor forsake thee.

*6 **Be strong and of a good courage:** for unto this people shalt thou divide for an inheritance the land, which I sware unto their fathers to give them.*

Leadership: You Can Have What It Takes

*7 Only **be thou strong and very courageous**, that thou mayest observe to do according to all the law, which Moses my servant commanded thee: turn not from it to the right hand or to the left, that thou mayest prosper whithersoever thou goest.*

8 This book of the law shall not depart out of thy mouth; but thou shalt meditate therein day and night, that thou mayest observe to do according to all that is written therein: for then thou shalt make thy way prosperous, and then thou shalt have good success.

9 Have I not commanded thee? ***be strong and of a good courage; be not afraid, neither be thou dismayed: for the LORD thy God is with thee whithersoever thou goest.*** (Joshua 1:1-9)

God is talking to Joshua about assuming the leadership of the nation of Israel after the death of Moses. Joshua is not inheriting an enviable position. Moses left very big shoes to fill. The nation was not known for its eagerness in following.

The Lord began to talk to Joshua, and told him to take the people into the promised land. Notice, **God, not the people, chose the leader.**

God assured Joshua that He would be with him even as He had been with Moses. He also told Joshua that he would be an effective leader. Mark all of the verses where God told Joshua to be strong and courageous, and not to be afraid.

Look at Joshua 1:8. It is God's Formula for Success.

Courage

This book of the law shall not depart out of thy mouth; but thou shalt meditate therein day and night, that thou mayest observe to do according to all that is written therein: for then thou shalt make thy way prosperous, and then thou shalt have good success. (Joshua 1:8)

God told Joshua to meditate on the Word day and night. By doing so, he would have success and would prosper. **If you want to be a leader, then you have to make this "Formula" an intergal part of your life.**

You will not enjoy success as a leader without doing what God told Joshua. There is no substitute for meditation in God's Word, and no short-cut to success in life. All of God's leaders have come by way of the advice of Joshua 1:8.

The word "meditate" means "to mutter or to speak to yourself in a low tone of voice." He said, by meditating, you will observe what to do and how to do it. Through meditating in the Word and speaking the Word to yourself, you will become enlightened. Your eyes will be open to what God's Word says for you to do. Then you can do it.

When you see what to do (through meditating), and when you do it, you will prosper and find good success.

I have this written in the front of my Bible: "Charles, if you are a failure, it is because you are too lazy to be a success. Joshua 1:8. The Law Of Success."

It is that simple. Anyone can do it.

Joshua was a tremendous man of God. He does not get as much attention as others in the Bible because he

Leadership: You Can Have What It Takes

lived in the shadow of Moses. The Bible says he was the greatest prophet who ever lived in the nation of Israel.

Moses brought the people right up to the banks of the Jordan river. When they arrived at the Jordan river, it was in flood stage. According to history, when the Jordan river flooded, it reached from two to five miles across.

The Lord spoke to Joshua and told him, "Joshua, Moses is dead."

I have always imagined Joshua thinking, "You don't have to tell me. If there is anybody in this camp who knows Moses is dead, it's me."

He realized that mantle of leadership was coming upon him. He had been hand-picked many years before for this time. He knew it, and everybody else knew it.

Joshua was standing at the banks of the Jordan river. Moses, the man who had experience with large bodies of water, is dead. There stood Joshua. He had watched Moses at the Red Sea. He saw the whole thing take place.

Now he is the leader. God hasn't said anything about getting a rod yet.

Did you ever think about that? Why didn't God let Joshua use a rod?

The rod didn't have anything to do with parting a body of water. The rod was merely a point of contact for Moses to release his faith.

Rememeber, Joshua was his own man. God does not want a carbon copy of Moses. Joshua must establish his own leadership identity. He cannot try to act like Moses, or do things exactly like Moses did. **He must be himself and allow God to use him as He pleases.**

Courage

They are at the bank of the Jordan river, and the Lord said to Joshua, "I want you to take these people across the river."

He told him that He was going to give Joshua the land. Every place his foot would tread would be his. God told him no man would be able to stand against him. That was good news to Joshua's ears. The Lord said, "As I was with Moses, I will be with you. I will not fail you nor forsake you." In verse six, God told Joshua to be strong and of good courage. In verse seven, God told him again, "... be thou strong and very courageous." And in verse nine, God said He had given Joshua a commandment. You might think it was to cross the Jordan river. But it wasn't. It was **to be strong and of good courage.**

Why did God command Joshua, His leader, to be strong and of good courage? Does courage play an important part in leadership?

Joshua needed to be courageous. And God was warning him that Satan would try to overwhelm him with fear.

You cannot be a leader without courage. Satan will send fear directly against your courage.

Satan knows there is absolutely nothing he can do to stop your faith, once you put it into motion. **You** can pull it back and stop it. But once **you** set your faith in motion, once **you** believe you have received, once **you** have set your stand on the Word of God, there is absolutely nothing Satan can throw against you that can stop your faith.

Jesus said...unto them, With men this is impossible; but with God all things are possible. (Matthew 19:26)

Above all, taking the shield of faith, wherewith ye shall be able to quench all the fiery darts of the wicked. (Ephesians 6:16)

That means there is nothing in Satan's arsenal that he can throw against your faith, which, of its own, can stop your faith. Once you get your faith in motion, there is not a problem big enough to overcome it.

There is not a financial need large enough that can overcome your faith. Your faith can overcome anything.

Why?

The faith that you now have in your heart came from hearing the Word of God. Faith comes from hearing the Word of God (Romans 10:17). This is how it works. You hear the Word. God's faith is in His Word. God put His faith into His Word. As you hear His Word, His faith gets into you. You then have His faith in you. You have the God kind of faith in your heart.

Whereby are given unto us exceeding great and precious promises: that by these ye might be partakers of the divine nature.... (2nd Peter 1:4)

22 But the fruit of the spirit is love, joy, peace, longsuffering, gentleness, goodness, faith,

23 Meekness, temperance.... (Galatians 5:22-23)

Jesus said in Mark 11:22-23, talking about the faith of God, that whoever shall believe in his heart that those things which he says shall come to pass, he shall have whatever he says--to such an extent that you can speak to a mountain, command it to be moved, and it will be cast into the sea.

Courage

From a natural standpoint, that is impossible. That mountain could be any number of things. It could be a physical need, a financial need, or an emotional need. But you can speak to it. You can use faith.

Where does faith come from?

It comes from hearing the Word of God. The word "hearing" in the Greek text has a verb tense called a continual tense. It would be convenient if we had this verb tense in English. Romans 10:17, in the Greek text, is, "faith comes by hearing, and hearing, and hearing, ..."

The continual tense indicates continual action. Once it is set into motion, it continues on and on.

It is not enough to hear the Word of God one time in your life. You must continue to hear it all of your life. If you are to remain strong spiritually, you must continue to hear the Word of God. You feed your body daily, and you must also feed yourself spiritually daily.

Romans 1:17 says that *The just shall live by faith.* The greek text says, "My righteous ones shall have their lives sustained by faith."

Faith is the sustaining force of the Christian life. Without it you will begin to wither.

You must discipline yourself to a steady diet of God's Word, or you will grow weak spiritually. This is especially important if you are in a leadership position, because there is a greater drain on your faith. Make sure you do not allow yourself to become spiritually anemic.

Satan can bring nothing against you to stop your faith from working. He knows, when you make a decision in your heart, faith is ignited in your spirit by the Word of

God. You release it out of your mouth through the Word that you speak in the form of a prayer or confession.

Once faith is released from your heart, nothing can stand in the way of your faith. It doesn't matter how it looks, or how hopeless it seems. Through the power of faith in God's Word, situations change.

A young man from Mexico came to one of our healing services. Eight months earlier, he had undergone surgery for a brain tumor. During the surgery, an optic nerve was cut, causing blindness. He was eighteen, and blind for the rest of his life.

He sat in the Spanish interpretation room. I laid hands on him and prayed, as I did for many others. I didn't know he was blind.

Later, while I was still praying for others, the interpreter brought him back to the platform. He began to explain what had taken place. When I prayed, nothing happened, but when he got back to his seat, he began to be able to distinguish colors and light.

I laid my hands on him and prayed again. His vision got clearer. I prayed another time and his vision got better. Before he left the service that evening, he was reading his Bible. Glory to the King!

Impossible situations can be changed by your faith in God's Word. Don't be afraid of the impossible. God commanded Joshua, *Be strong and of a good courage; be not afraid.*

I have discovered why fear comes against you. It comes to stop your faith. It stops your faith by attacking your courage.

Courage

Courage is the quality of mind or spirit that enables a person to face difficulty, danger, pain with firmness, without fear, with bravery. You must have courage in your mind and in your spirit.

A family in our church had been through tremendous turmoil. During this time, the lady of the house had been burned very severely by a fire bomb that had exploded in her bed.

When I saw her in the hospital bed, something on the inside of me tried to lie down. It was my courage. My faith was strong. But I just could not seem to get from the doorway to the bed to pray for her.

Fear came to snatch away my courage. Courage is that quality which enables you to face difficulty, instead of turning and running. You cannot convince faith that it can't do something. But the devil will try to put a stranglehold on your courage.

Be wise enough to watch out for fear when it tries to get hold of you. If you know it's going to come, don't let it get in you. **Be prepared** for it. Don't believe for it.

Sometimes God is going to bring you into life or death situations where you are the man or the woman who is going to make the difference. Do your very best. Be prepared. People deserve the best. They have a right to expect it from the body of Christ.

I spoke to fear and said, "You lying devil, you get out of here in Jesus' name."

I knew in my heart that God would heal her. I was convinced of it. I also knew that fear was trying to come against me. I made myself walk across the room, and I prayed for her and spoke life to her skin.

Leadership: You Can Have What It Takes

In six weeks she was out of the hospital, totally healed, delivered, and set free--with no scars. The skin began to supernaturally come back. No skin graft was needed. The doctor said it was a miracle. Faith in God's Word produced that miracle.

The Word of God is more than enough. Medical science was not enough in her case. It took supernatural, miracle-working power from God to restore that woman's flesh. That never would have happened if I had allowed fear to quench my courage.

You must have faith. You cannot live without it.

At times, you will face situations when fear will come. The devil knows, when you activate faith in your heart, he cannot stop you. He will try to keep you from ever using your faith. He will attempt to steal your courage.

Did you know that you already have courage because you are a partaker of God's divine nature? There is that quality in your spirit that will enable you to face problems.

You will not receive from God, if you think He can meet your need, but believe He probably won't. If there is anything God requires out of you, it is one hundred percent commitment to His Word.

Satan will tell you that you are not going to make it; the problem is too big. Don't settle for his lies. Don't waver between faith and unbelief. Stand by your commitment to the Word of God.

Have not I commanded thee? Be strong and of a good courage; be not afraid, neither be thou dismayed: for the LORD thy God is with thee whithersoever thou goest. (Joshua 1:9)

Here is something you need to know about your courage. This is the thing that pumps up your courage--**God is with you.**

That is what Joshua needed to hear--"God is with me." By yourself you can do nothing, but with Him you can do all things (Philippians 4:13).

Joshua came to the people and walked through the middle of them, commanding the officers, saying, "Pass through the host, and command the people, saying, Prepare your food and get everything ready, for in three days we're going to pass over this Jordan river."

He didn't have any idea how. All he knew was that his courage was pumped up. He had been feeding on the fact that God almighty, El Shaddai, the God Who is more than enough, the God Who split the Red Sea is with him! Who cares about the Jordan river? He said they were going into the land to possess it. He talked to the Reubenites, the Gadites, and to the half tribe of Manasseh, saying they could stay on the other side of the Jordan river. They wanted that land, and God told them through Moses that they could stay. That was their portion of the promised land, but they would have to help the other tribes possess their portions.

Joshua told them, "Remember, Moses said that you can have this land."

14 Your wives, your little ones, and your cattle, shall remain in the land which Moses gave you on this side Jordan; but ye shall pass before your brethren armed, all the mighty men of valour, and help them;

15 Until the LORD have given your brethren rest, as he hath given you, and they also have posessed the land which the LORD your God giveth them: then ye shall return unto the land of your possession, and enjoy it, which Moses the LORD's servant gave you on this side Jordan toward the sunrising. (Joshua 1:14-15)

The people agreed this was the fair thing to do.

Joshua was exerting himself as their leader. He was taking his God-given position. But the people must still accept him.

You cannot lead if people will not follow. The things he said to the Reubenites, the Gadites, and the half-tribe of Manasseh had already been said by Moses. They were things they could agree upon.

But would they accept his instructions to prepare to cross the Jordan river? If they did, would there be any limitations to his leadership? Look how they answered him.

And they answered Joshua, saying, All that thou commandest us we will do, and whithersoever thou sendest us, we will go. (Joshua 1:16)

Remember, they were still on the other side of the swollen Jordan river. Their leader said they would pass over to the other side.

Study the attitude of the people. We need to get it into our hearts. They did not stand there and question him. They did what he said to do.

Courage

They told him three things they expected of him as their leader. These are the same things people expect today..

According as we hearkened unto Moses in all things, so will we harken unto thee: only the LORD thy God be with thee, as he was with Moses. (Joshua 1:17)

The first thing they required was that the anointing of God be upon his life. If you are going to be a leader, then people have a right to expect God's anointing to be upon you.

They expected to see God with Joshua, just as He was with Moses. To be a leader, you must spend the time it takes in prayer and study of God's Word for God's anointing to come upon you. You cannot lead only by idea or causes. You must have God's anointing.

Whosoever he be that doth rebel against thy commandment, and will not hearken unto thy words in all that thou commandest him, he shall be put to death: only be strong and of a good courage. (Joshua 1:18)

I am not recommending that for today. I am pointing out the serious approach of commitment these men took toward Joshua.

Look at the next two things they told Joshua. "Only be strong and of good courage." People expect their leaders to be strong and courageous. Sometimes you set goals and plans to fulfill your vision. When you begin to run with it, you ask God, "Am I expecting too much? Am I going too far? Am I doing too much? Am I putting too much upon the people?"

Leadership: You Can Have What It Takes

I asked myself this, and the Lord said, "No, you are not."

The people expect their leaders to be strong and of good courage. They want their leaders to face up to difficulties. This is one of the greatest things I have learned about leadership.

The people of Joshua's day and the people of today are not different. The Israelites expected their leaders to be strong and courageous. The people we face today desire the same thing.

I know how easy it is to talk yourself out of doing great things for God, and be content with mediocrity. Do not let that happen.

Often, thoughts of fear have come into my mind, telling me that my vision to win my city to the kingdom of God is too big, and if I shared it with my congregation they would run away. I have found the exact opposite to be true of my congregation and other groups of believers. People want their leaders to be strong and courageous.

Do not be afraid to put your vision before your people. But use wisdom concerning how much you tell them. Always make sure that every project you give your people to do, you follow through until it is completed. Do not make a habit of starting projects you cannot finish or do not finish. You will lose credibility as a leader.

I have also seen people in positions of authority take off on something, when they should have waited and compiled more information before beginning.

Any enterprise is built by wise planning, becomes strong through common sense, and profits wonderfully by keeping abreast of the facts. (Proverbs 24:3-4 Living)

Being called by God, anointed, and living by faith does not give us the right or license to fail to plan wisely, use common sense, and keep abreast of the facts.

For some reason, many believers put aside these principles when they start walking with the Lord.

Don't make these mistakes. We must be courageous. But being courageous does not mean being weird.

Make a habit of surveying every situation you are in. Do not make decisions out of fear.

Remember Joshua. He had a problem and waited until he received the Lord's advice on what to do. When you have God's Word concerning a situation, then you can be courageous, because you know how everything will turn out.

Chapter II

THE ORIGINS OF FEAR

Fear will short-circuit your faith. Every time the nation of Israel was facing a problem, God instructed them in how to overcome the problem. The first thing He said to them was, *Fear not.* Before He told Joshua what to do, before He told Moses what to do, before He told anyone what to do, He told them to *Fear not.* Then He gave them their instructions.

Why did He tell them to "Fear not" before He gave them their instructions?

If He gave them the instructions while there was fear in their heart, fear would cause them to fail, even when they obeyed the instructions.

Fear will short-circuit the effectiveness of God's Word in your heart. Before you can see God's promises fulfilled in your life, you must get fear out and get faith in.

26 And God said, Let us make man in our image, after our likeness: and let them have dominion over the fish of the sea, and over the fowl of the air, and over the cattle, and over all the earth, and over every creeping thing that creepeth upon the earth. (Genesis 1:26)

And God said, Let us make man in our image.... Notice the word "us" and "our." Those are plural words, revealing there was more than one being present when God spoke. We know that those beings were the Father, Son and Holy Ghost.

There is one major religious group in America which does not believe that. They believe that the "us" and the "our" were the angels. That is ridiculous, because angels **do not** have creative ability.

Whoever was standing there with God at that time had the same creative ability that God did. They were in God's own image. They looked like Him and acted like Him. He said, *Let us make man in our image....* We know that was the Father, Son and Holy Ghost.

...and let them (man) *have dominion....* Dominion is the right and the power to govern and control. When you have the right and the power to govern and control, you have dominion. Let me give you an illustration that I believe will help you understand it better.

The Shah of Iran had the right to govern and control. It was his by birth. But he did not have the power. Hitler had the power, but he did not have the right.

God gave the right and the power—the right and the power to govern and control—to man. He gave them dominion.

The Origins Of Fear

What did He give them dominion over? *...And let them have dominion over the fish of the sea, and over the fowl of the air, and over the cattle, and over all the earth....*

How much of the earth did they have dominion over? All of it.

...and over every creeping thing that creepeth upon the earth. As Charles Capps has said, "God has even given you dominion over creeps."

27 So God created man in his own image, in the image of God created he him; male and female created he them. (Genesis 1:27)

Many people believe that there is the man, and then there is the woman. You hear them say, "Well, you know, God created everyone equal."

But they don't act that way. They don't let it operate that way in the churches. It is not that way in reality.

He said that God created man, male and female. Man is one species with two types. The species is man, the types are male and female.

28 And God blessed them, (male and female), *and God said unto them, Be fruitful, and multiply, and replenish the earth, and subdue it: and have dominion* (God gave dominion to male and female--He gave them both the right and power to govern and control) *over the fish of the sea, and over the fowl of the air, and over every living thing that moveth* (or creeps) *upon the earth.* (Genesis 1:28)

God gave Adam and Eve dominion--the right and the power to govern and control everything that moved upon this planet. That included Satan.

15 And the LORD God took the man, (that should read Adam, the male), *and put him into the garden of Eden to dress it and to keep it.* (Genesis 2:15)

The Hebrew text for the word "keep" means "guard." God turned to Adam and said, "Adam I'm putting you in the garden of Eden to do two two things. You are here to take care of it, and you are here to guard it."

Many people have heard the story of Adam and Eve in the garden of Eden. They are under the impression that God put Adam and Eve in the garden like little babes in the woods, so innocent and pure and holy. They were cruising through the woods and enjoying the flowers and the bugs and the birds and the lions. Just kind of floating along. And then suddenly, one day a snake came up, and they ate the fruit. And then God dropped the whole world on them.

But that is not what happened.

The very fact that God told Adam to guard the garden reveals to us that Adam knew there was somebody there who might try to steal what Adam had. Why do they have security guards in factories? They are there because there is a possibilitiy that someone might try to come in and steal or damage something.

A security guard is there to keep that from happening. God told Adam to guard the garden. God gave him the right and the authority or power to govern and control everything that moved on the planet. Adam was well aware that there was an enemy, a thief on the planet, and God gave him the right and the power to control him.

The Origins Of Fear

16 And the LORD God commanded the man, saying, Of every tree of the garden thou mayest freely eat:

17 But of the tree of the knowledge of good and evil, thou shalt not eat of it: for in the day that thou eatest thereof thou shalt surely die. (Genesis 2:16-17)

The word **surely** means "of a guarantee." God guaranteed Adam that if he ate of the fruit of the tree of the knowledge of good and evil, he would die. It is one thing to get a guarantee from General Motors or General Electric, but it is something else to get a guarantee from God. When God said, "I guarantee it, you will die," you are going to die. There are no ifs, no ands, no maybes, no mights. You will die.

They ate the fruit. They did not fall over and die. They lived nine hundred more years. But God said in the day you eat you shall surely die.

What kind if death was He talking about?

To understand this, you must read the literal Hebrew text. It says, "in dying you shall surely die," revealing that two deaths would take place.

In dying one death, you shall surely die another death. One death would occur when they ate it, and another death would come later—revealing that two deaths would take place.

The first death was spiritual, and the second death was physical death. They would die first spiritually, and then later physically. We know that they did eat and they did die, but they did not die physically.

Isaiah fifty-three says that Jesus became one with us in death. The Hebrew text says "deaths." He died twice. He died spiritually, and then he died physically. That had to occur so Jesus would become one with us the way we were, so we could be one with Him the way He was going to be.

18 And the LORD God said, It is not good that the man should be alone; I will make him an help meet for him. (Genesis 2:18)

Notice in Genesis 1:31 God had finished with creation, it was the end of the sixth day.

And God saw every thing that he had made, and, behold, it was very good.... (Genesis 1:31)

When He was done with creation He saw that it was very good. However, there was a time during creation when it was not good. Genesis 2:18 said that *...it is not good that the man should be alone....* The word "alone" in the Hebrew text is an interesting word. Occasionally, one Hebrew word will require a whole sentence of English words to translate it.

In the Hebrew language, instead of making new words, they simply add a letter to an existing word to change the meaning of that word. The literal text reads like this, *And the Lord God said that Adam's strength should not be spread out in this way.* That is what the word "alone" means.

We could say it like this, "Adam is spread too thin. He has too much responsibility, too much to do, too much to watch over, too many things to take care of. There is too much going on. It is not good. He is spread too thin.

His strength is spread out too much. It is not good that Adam's strength should be spread out in this way."

So He said, *I will make him an help meet for him.* (Genesis 2:18b) It does not say help mate. I says help meet. There is a big difference between a helpmeet and helpmate. Once again, the Hebrew text reads like this, *I will make a helper for Adam. I will make someone to help Adam like Adam, is helping Me.*

Remember that Adam was made in the image and in the likeness of God. God breathed the breath of life into Adam. He had the very nature and the likeness of God inside of him, and this creature that God was going to make for Adam was going to be exactly like Adam. This creature would be made in his image, in his likeness. It would not be above him, it would not be below him. It would stand equal with him.

Many people tend to think that God suddenly lost track of what He was doing and went off on a tangent for a couple of days making animals. *And the LORD God said, It is not good that the man's strength should be spread out in this way; I will make someone to help him like he has been helping Me.*

19 And out of the ground the LORD God formed every beast of the field, and every fowl of the air; and brought them unto Adam to see what he would call them: and whatsoever Adam called every living creature, that was the name thereof.

20 And Adam gave names to all cattle, and to the fowl of the air, and to every beast of the field; but for Adam there was not found an help meet for him. (someone to help him like he was helping God.) (Genesis 2:19-20)

To paraphrase what God said, "Adam's life is not good, so I am going to make someone to help him. I am going to make someone who will help him, who is totally in his class, who has his abilities. This creature will be able to help Adam as much as Adam is helping me."

Remember, when God made Adam, He made him in His own likeness after His own image. He did not make man to crawl around in the dirt and come before God to say, "Oh, I'm so unworthy, I'm no good." He made Adam so Adam could stand in the presence of God and feel at home. Then we see that God began to make beasts of the field. God said He was going to make Adam a helper, and he started to make the beasts of the field.

Notice God's first attempt at finding the helper for Adam was the animal kingdom. He formed them out of the dust of the ground and brought them before Adam to see what Adam would call them. Adam gave every one of them names.

This shows us something about Adam's mental capabilities. He was a smart fellow. However, the animals were not what the Lord had in mind. Notice the word "but" in verse 21. God was going to move in another direction, or a change was coming. The Word says, *...but for Adam there was not found an help meet....* The word "but" shows us that the first attempt God made to bring Adam a helper was in the animal kingdom. But they did not do what God wanted. Though the animals were good, they did not accomplish what was needed.

21 And the LORD God caused a deep sleep to fall upon Adam, and he slept: and he took one of his ribs, and closed up the flesh instead thereof;

22 And the rib, which the LORD God had taken from man, made he a woman, and brought her unto the man.

23 And Adam said, This is now bone of my bones, and flesh of my flesh.... (Genesis 2:21-23)

The Hebrew text reads like this, "At last this one is bone of my bone." Adam knew what the problem was. God knew what the problem was. They both knew that the problem with the animals was that they were not bone of Adam's bone and flesh of Adam's flesh. They were not in Adam's class. They were not of his same nature.

The only way this helper would be able to meet the needs in Adam's life and stand with him would be if it was equal with him, bone of his bone and flesh of his flesh; not beneath him, and not above him. The first moment Adam looked at her, he said, "At last, this one is bone of my bone and flesh of my flesh. And she shall be called woman."

The literal word is "womb-man," revealing that the woman came from man. That is not a put-down, it's a statement of fact. That statement was not given as a hammer in man's hand to hold over the woman. If the gospel had been preached in America the way it should have been preached, there never would have been an equal rights movement.

If you study history, you will discover that Jesus was the first world religious teacher who ever addressed women as anything other than property. He was the only one who ever addressed them as being equal. Jesus is the great liberator of mankind.

23 And Adam said, This is now bone of my bones, and flesh of my flesh: she shall be called Woman, because she was taken out of Man.

24 Therefore (because of this) *shall a man leave his father and his mother, and shall cleave unto his wife: and they shall be one flesh.* (Genesis 2:23-24)

He said, *Therefore* (because of this) *shall a man leave his father and his mother, and shall cleave unto his wife: and they shall be one flesh.*

Because of what?

Because God *took one of his ribs, and closed up the flesh instead thereof.* (v.28)

When God made Adam, He made him just the way He wanted him; and then He took a rib out of his side. If God put that rib in Adam to begin with, then He must have intended for him to have that rib from the beginning.

The natural train of thought would have been for the Lord to take the rib out and then create another one. But He did not. He *closed up the flesh instead thereof* and left Adam one rib short. He took the rib and built this woman and brought her to Adam; a love gift from God to Adam.

Adam looked at her and said, "At last! This one is bone of my bone and flesh of my flesh."

Adam looked down and saw the scar on his own side, looked up and said, Because of this--because a part of me which God had put in me in the beginning to make me

The Origins Of Fear

whole and complete is now in her--a man shall leave his father and mother, and he shall cleave unto his wife so they can become one."

He is basically saying, for the male to find fulfillment of himself, he will find the woman that God gives him, and they will become one. The man shall find fulfillment of himself in the woman that God has given him.

While Adam is still talking, he begins to prophesy. We know this, because every time God speaks or prophesies, He always says, "And the Lord said...." He does not leave it to chance for you to know who is talking.

24 Therefore shall a man leave his father and his mother, and shall cleave unto his wife: and they shall be one flesh. (Genesis 2:24)

Adam is speaking of things he has no knowledge of, things that can only come to him by the Spirit of God speaking through him. Adam has no knowledge of mothers or fathers. He doesn't know what a mother or a father is.

It was the Spirit of God in him speaking through him. Adam spoke about what was going to be the natural course of events in human lives from that day to this day. Men are still leaving their parents to be joined unto their wives.

The Bible says that man would "cleave unto his wife." That is an interesting thought. It is very foreign to our way of thinking. In most marriages today, we see the exact opposite. We have the big, macho husband allowing the poor weak wife the privilege of living with him under his protection.

Leadership: You Can Have What It Takes

Society and the church have put men and women into roles that neither one can handle. I believe that is one of the reasons for the massive failure in marriages in the world today.

Women were not made by God as men's servants, and men were not made to be the rulers of women. At the same time, men were not made to be ruled by women, and women were not made to rule men. They were made as equals! Together they were to rule the earth and everything that moved upon it (Genesis 1:26-28).

It is interesting that Adam said man would cleave to his wife. For some reason, in our society today, few men will admit that they need their wives. Some men will not allow themselves to become close to their wives nor let their wives become close to them. They always maintain a wall between them. That is a shame and a great loss.

It is not a sign of weakness for a man to need and lean on the strength of his wife. In fact, it is a sign of strength that comes from wisdom. Do not misunderstand what I am saying. I do not believe in hen-pecked husbands any more than I believe in bullied, suppressed wives. I believe in Bible equality—the man and the woman drawing strength from one another. That is the way God intended it to be.

Remember, God did not take a bone from Adam's foot to make the woman. If He had, men would have said, "That means women are beneath men." He also did not take a bone from Adam's head, which women would have interpreted as meaning that women were to be over men.

No! He took a rib from Adam's side, which symbolizes equality. Eve was in Adam's class—spirit, soul, and body.

The Origins Of Fear

To be a supernatural leader, we must understand this. Many people today are constantly in competition with their own husband or wife. Needless to say, no one will follow these people. We must allow God to put our marriage in proper perspective.

Now the serpent was more subtil than any beast of the field which the Lord God had made. And he said unto the woman, Yea, hath God said, Ye shall not eat of every tree of the garden? (Genesis 3:1)

When Satan comes against you in your life, he will never come ringing a bell. He will slide up to you just like a snake in the grass. "subtil" means "sneaky." The Hebrew text reads, "Yes, God has said you shall not eat of every tree of the garden. Why?"

You need to understand that the fall of man was a moral issue. Satan was not questioning what God said. He questioned God's reason for saying it. You will notice in the next verses that Eve answered the question correctly. But Satan was able to plant the seed of doubt in Eve's mind that God had an ulterior motive in telling them not to eat the fruit of the tree of the knowledge of good and evil.

2 And the woman said unto the serpent, We may eat of the fruit of the trees of the garden:

3 But of the fruit of the tree which is in the midst of the garden, God hath said, Ye shall not eat of it, neither shall ye touch it, lest ye die. (Genesis 3:2-3)

He said, "Why has God said you can't eat of that fruit?"

She answered, "Because we will die."

She gave him the right answer. If she gave him the right answer, then why did she end up falling?

She did not stand on the right answer. She did not build her house on the rock. She got on the rock, but his answer knocked her off. When she got off of the rock, she was washed away. Just being on the rock does not mean that you are going to stay on the rock. The waves will come up and hit that rock.

And the serpent said unto the woman, Ye shall not surely die. (Genesis 3:4)

There you are, Eve. You have a choice. Did God mean what He said?

That was the question before Eve, and that is question before us.

Once while I was reading this verse, ...*Ye shall not surely die,* the Lord said to me, "That is why the lion roars." He was referring to First Peter 5:8, which says that Satan goes about as a roaring lion, seeking whom he may devour.

It is interesting that the Lord used that illustration, because just a few nights before, I had watched a special on public television about a pride of lions. The lioness was hunting at a water hole. She would lie in the high grass next to the water hole, motionless, waiting for hours.

She would wait until an antelope or gazelle (which by itself had the speed and ability to outrun her) got within her grasp. When it was close enough, she would rise up and let out an ear-splitting roar. The roar would circle the water hole, and those animals could not tell where she was hiding. They would stand there, shaking

The Origins Of Fear

and trembling. Then the lioness would run out, jump on her prey, kill it, and take it back to eat.

Why did the lioness roar?

She roared because it paralyzed her victims with fear. Satan goes about as a roaring lion, seeking whom he may devour. He roars the same thing in our ears today that he did in Eve's ear—"The Word is not true."

God said they would die, and Satan said that was not true. The devil will roar in your ear, "No, the Word is not true. What God says is not true."

When you get over that hurdle, you will whip him.

How do you get over that hurdle?

Decide. Make a decision in your heart that, as a free moral agent upon this planet, you have the right to decide what you are going to believe. Then choose to believe what is written in the Bible. Look at him and say, "Devil, I believe it."

Satan cannot stop you from making a decision.

All leaders must be able to make decisions. You cannot vacillate and expect people to follow you.

For God doth know that in the day ye eat thereof, then your eyes shall be opened, and ye shall be as gods, knowing good and evil. (Genesis 3:5)

It is very interesting that the devil is telling Eve what God knows—and he is still doing the same thing today. He has not changed one bit. He is constantly challenging believers' minds regarding what they believe to be God's methods of doing things, and His reasons for doing them.

He has managed to get some believers to think that God uses the devil to teach the church.

God and the devil are not working together to make you a better person. We need to get our minds renewed to this. We must get out or our false humility trip and get into reality.

What is false humility?

So often you will find believers who believe that everything happening in their life, good or bad, is the work of the Lord to make them better people. They say things like, "Well, I'm a Christian, and because of that, everything that happens in my life must be from the Lord. Therefore, If I get sick, or lose my job, or get in a car wreck, the Lord is just trying to teach me something. And even though I don't know why these things are happening to me when I've been such a good person, I will just keep on loving the Lord anyway. Even though it doesn't seem fair what God is doing to me, I will stay true to Him and love Him."

All of that sounds beautiful and wonderful and humble. There is only one thing wrong with that type of thinking—IT IS WRONG! God does not use bad things to teach His children. There is no place in the Bible where scripture even hints of that.

Let no man say when he is tempted, I am tempted of God: for God cannot be tempted with evil, neither tempteth he any man. (James 1:13)

The word "tempt" can also be translated "tested or tried." God does not use temptations, tests, or trials to teach His people.

The Origins Of Fear

Where do they come from then?

The thief cometh not, but for to steal, and to kill, and to destroy: I am come that they might have life, and that they might have it more abundantly. (John 10:10)

Satan, not God, is the one who authors evil things in believers' lives. We must get this straight once and for all in our thinking and believing. If not, we will be confused, and the people we are leading will be confused.

Jesus came to give us abundant life—not sickness, disease, poverty, fear, torment, want, depression, etc. but **abundant life.** God and the devil are not in league together to make you a better person. God does not use the devil to teach the church. The job of teaching the church is the Holy Spirit's responsibility.

But the Comforter, which is the Holy Ghost, whom the Father will send in my name, he shall teach you all things, and bring all things to your remembrance, whatsoever I have said unto you. (John 14:26)

Knowing good and evil does not make you a god. Satan knew good and evil, and it did not make him a god. It made him a loser.

And when the woman saw that the tree was good for food, and that it was pleasant to the eyes, and a tree to be desired to make one wise, she took of the fruit thereof, and did eat, and gave also unto her husband with her; and he did eat. (Genesis 3:6)

Adam was standing there, and he saw the whole thing. He was not somewhere else in the garden naming bugs. The Bible says the woman was deceived, but the man was not.

And Adam was not deceived, but the woman being deceived was in the transgression. (1st Timothy 2:14)

Have you ever wondered why the sin that occurred in the Garden was called the sin of Adam? Eve ate the fruit first. Why wasn't it called the sin of Eve? Satan deceived Eve.

The word "deceived" means "to be mislead by false appearance." Satan misled her. He made her think something was other than it really was.

On the other hand, Adam entered into it with his eyes open wide. He was not deceived. Adam was a spiritual creature. He was a man; he had flesh and bone just like we have. He also had a soul. But he was so conscious of living in the spiritual realm that he did not realize he was without clothes. There was a glory that came forth from him because he was in he presence of God and he had the breath and life of God in him.

Can you imagine getting so full of the things of God and so knowledgeable in the Word of God that you get up and go to town and leave your pants at home?

Adam watched Eve take the fruit and eat it. God said they would die if they ate of that fruit. Adam watched Eve die. Then Adam reached up and took the fruit and ate it himself.

Why did Adam sin when he had witnessed the consequences?

He wanted to. He did it for the same reason that men from that day to this day have known things were wrong, and did them anyway—because they wanted to.

The Origins Of Fear

7 And the eyes of them both were opened, and they knew that they were naked; (the word "naked" in the Hebrew text means "disarmed") *and they sewed fig leaves together, and made themselves aprons.*

8 And they heard the voice of the Lord God walking in the garden in the cool of the day: and Adam and his wife hid themselves from the presence of the LORD God amongst the trees of the garden. (Genesis 3:7-8)

Notice that Adam and Eve tried to hide from the Lord among the trees of the garden. Did Adam think the Lord wouldn't know where he was? Maybe he thought God was going to walk on the planet and say, "You know, this looks like earth. I could have sworn this was earth, but I guess it's not—Adam isn't here."

We all know that God knew where Adam was. If He knew where he was, Why did the Lord ask Adam, "Where art thou?"

God asked Adam where he was for the same reason you say, "Son, where are you?" when you walk into your child's room and see drawings all over the wall, and you hear the little guy breathing in the closet. You know where he is.

Why did you ask him?

Because you want him to answer for his disobedience. God is dealing with his disobedient son.

And he said, I heard thy voice in the garden, and I was afraid.... (Genesis 3:10)

There is fear. This is the first time for the human race that fear came into existence. It began in man's relation-

39

ship with God. The first trace of fear was man's fear toward God. That fear is still in the earth today.

FACTS ABOUT FEAR

Fear is a spiritual force. It is not an emotion, although it will affect your emotions. It is not a feeling, although it will give you some feelings. Fear is a spiritual force. Faith is the power force of the kingdom of God. It will go forth into the kingdom of God to lay hold upon the things that you desire in that kingdom, bringing them to you and making them a reality in your life.

Fear is the power force of the kingdom of darkness. It will go forth into the kingdom of darkness, lay hold upon the things that you are afraid of, and bring them to you, making them a reality in your life.

For the thing which I greatly feared is come upon me, and that which I was afraid of is come unto me. (Job 3:25)

Fear came forth out of his heart. His fear went forth into the spiritual realm and laid hold upon the things he was afraid of and brought them to him, making them a reality in his life. Fear is a spiritual force. It can be used, and developed, and spread from one person to another. Fear can be transmitted from me to you. It can pass from one member of a family to another; from one family to another; from one community to another; from one city to another; from one state to another; from one nation to another, to the entire world.

Franklin D. Roosevelt made this statement when our nation was facing one of the most critical points in her history.

The Origins Of Fear

He said, "We have nothing to fear but fear itself."

He had the insight to realize that if America was to get back up on her feet, she had to overcome fear.

Fear will paralyze you. It will stop you from doing things that you know you should do, or know you can do.

Fear will paralyze you in your walk with God, in your relationship with the Lord, in your receiving from God, in your marriage, on your job, in your relationships with other people, and in your family.

Fear is a terrible thing to let loose into a family. It is a terrible thing, and it bears terrible fruit. It is a wicked, wicked thing. There is no place for it in the human heart.

WIRED FOR FAITH

You have been wired for faith, not fear. Do you know what happens if you take an appliance that has been wired for AC current and plug it into DC current? Something is going to give way. It is not going to work.

Do you know what happens when you, wired for faith, are plugged into fear? Something will give way. You begin breaking down and coming apart at the seams. First a little at a time, and them completely, if you do not get control of it.

Fear is a spiritual force, and it is a powerful force. With fear in your heart, the Word of God will not work.

I will be teaching you in chapters to come how to get the fear out and the faith in. We will learn what the fruits of fear are, and what the Bible says fear will produce in your life. I will prove to you scripturally that fear will produce sickness, bondage, failure, torment, and ultimately death. Fear is not merciful. It will slowly kill you. It will eat you up from the inside out.

For God hath not given us the spirit of fear; but of power, and of love, and of a sound mind.
(2nd Timothy 1:7)

God has given us a spirit of power, a spirit of love, and a spirit of a sound mind. These three things are not listed by chance. If there are any three things that fear attacks in your life, it is your power, your love, and the soundness of your mind.

The Bible says that God has not given you the spirit of fear. Since God has not given you the spirit of fear, you do not have to have it. If He had given it to you, then you would have been stuck with it. But He did not give it to you. God has not given you the spirit of fear, but He has given you the spirit of power and of love and of a sound mind.

When you get fear out of your life, you will have power, you will have love, and you will have a sound mind. God has placed these three things inside of you.

Satan comes to steal, to kill, and to destroy (John 10:10). He comes to steal your power. He comes to steal your love. He comes to steal the soundness of your mind. He does not want your mind to be sound. He wants your mind to be full of bad dreams and images so that you can not think clearly—so you are unable to function in the earth.

That is Satan's plan. That is his plan for your life.

Jesus said He came so that you might have life and have it more abundantly. The word "life" in John 10:10 in the Greek text is the word "zoe," which means "life

The Origins Of Fear

like God has it." Jesus said, "I have come so that you can have life like God has it; that you might have the God kind of life; that you might live like God lives."

God has always desired for men to live like He does. We see that desire expressed in the Bible from Genesis through Revelation.

God is in control, and He wants men to be in control. He is in control of the universe, and mankind is in control on the earth. God gave man dominion. Dominion is the right and power to govern and control. It is your God-given right to live a life full of power, to live a life of love, and to have a sound mind.

Fear came into the human race in the garden of Eden when Adam and Eve committed the sin of high treason. The faith that was in them turned into fear. The confidence they had towards God was replaced with fear.

After they sinned, the Bible says they heard the voice of the Lord God walking in the garden in the cool of the day, and they tried to hide themselves from the Lord among the trees of the garden.

Fear will make you do dumb, stupid things. You cannot reason with someone who has fear in his heart. There is no reasoning with fear. Medical science has figured that out. Most good doctors will not operate on people when they are afraid. They will do everything they can to comfort them and quiet them down.

I read one research study which said that seventy-five percent of the people in hospitals today are there because of worry, tension, and fear. Can you imagine how many millions of dollars are being spent every year because people are afraid? Fear will eat you up.

Leadership: You Can Have What It Takes

Faith is the power force of the kingdom of God. It will go forth from your heart to lay hold upon the things that you desire in the kingdom of God, bringing them to you, and making them a reality in your life.

Fear is the power force of the kingdom of darkness. It will go forth from your heart to lay hold upon the things that you are afraid of, bringing them to you and making them a reality in your life.

Faith is a power force, and fear is a power force. They can be used and they can be developed. Only seven percent of the people in Russia actually belong to the Communist Party. Those seven percent control the other ninety-three percent with fear. They do not control them with guns and bullets and bombs. They control their people with fear.

Fear can be transmitted from one person to another. The Word says, *take heed what ye hear.* (Mark 4:24) You need to be careful about what you are listening to. Fear disrupts the soundness of your mind.

You need to understand this. You are never in neutral. You are either in unbelief, or you are in belief, but you are never in nonbelief. Unbelief is nonbelief. Unbelief is believing the wrong things. You are always believing something. If you yield to faith, you will overcome; if you yield to fear, you will go under.

The Lord once said to me, "Son, fear will attract demon spirits like blood attracts sharks." Man has discovered that some species of sharks can pick up the scent of blood in water a mile away, and they will follow that scent right to the thing that is bleeding. They come to destroy whatever it is that is bleeding. Blood in the water is a sign of helplessness.

Have you ever seen blood hit water? It spreads like a cloud. Think of fear like that. Fear comes out of your heart, goes into the spiritual realm, and spreads like a cloud. The demon spirits that are in the spiritual realm will pick up on that fear and follow it to whomever is afraid. Then they will wait to find out what the person is afraid of. He or she will tell them.

Why?

Because Jesus said out of the abundance of your heart your mouth will speak. (Matthew 12:34) You will tell them what you are afraid of, and they will go out and see to it that the thing you are afraid of comes to pass, just like it came to pass in Job's life.

PLANTING THE SEED OF FEAR

Satan uses four methods to try to get the seed of fear into your heart, where it will energize and bring forth fruit.

METHOD NUMBER ONE - WORDS. Words will be spoken to you in one or two ways, either by another person or by demonic spirits that speak directly into your consciousness. *...And Tobiah sent letters to put me in fear.* (Nehemiah 6:19) Nehemiah knew what Tobiah was trying to do and did not fall for his plan. Many times, words of fear will be spoken to you by well-meaning, sincere Christians who happen to be sincerely wrong.

How do you know when the devil is talking to you? When you hear these words: "but," "what if," and "how is God going to do that for you?" God does not talk in "buts," "what if's" and "hows." At times you may have thoughts that sound like this: "But what if the money doesn't get here on time?"

Leadership: You Can Have What It Takes

"How is the Lord going to do that for you?"

"What if you don't get healed when they pray for you? What then?"

Those are questions designed to plant the seed of fear in your heart. Once, in my own life, I was facing what seemed to be an insurmountable problem. I felt like the devil had me you going to meet this need?"

His reply changed my life when He said, "Charles, **the how** is not your care or responsibility. **The how** is My responsibility. Your responsibility is to believe the Word. My responsibility is to bring it to pass."

Glory be to God!

I turned to the devil and told him what I had just heard, and he became very quiet! From that day to this day, I have never worried about the **hows** of God's solutions.

Remember, the Bible says all the promises of God are "yes" and "so be it."

METHOD NUMBER TWO - SATAN WILL TRY TO SCARE YOU WITH THE SIZE OF THE PROBLEM. The Lord knew this and showed this to Israel in His laws concerning war, found in Deuteronomy.

> *1 When thou goest out to battle against thine enemies, and seest horses, and chariots, and a people more that thou, be not afraid of them: for the Lord thy GOD is with thee, which brought thee up out of the land of Egypt.*
>
> *2 And it shall be, when ye are come nigh unto the battle, that the priest shall approach and speak unto the people,*

The Origins Of Fear

3 And shall say unto them, Hear, O Israel, ye approach this day unto battle against your enemies: let not your hearts faint, fear not, and do not tremble, neither be ye terrified because of them;

4 For the LORD your God is he that goeth with you, to fight for you against your enemies, to save you.

8 And the officers shall speak further unto the people, and they shall say, What man is there that is fearful and faint-hearted? let him go and return unto his house, lest his brethren's heart faint as well as his heart. (Deuteronomy 20:1-4,8)

Fear can be transmitted from one person to another. For that reason, He said for the officers to tell everyone who was afraid to go home.

Gideon realized this, with the Lord's help. Gideon started out with thirty thousand men. That may sound like a lot of people. It isn't, when the army you are going to fight is so large that the Bible says they could not even number the campfires, and there were eight to ten men around each fire.

The first day, God told Gideon to tell everyone who was afraid to go home. Twenty thousand of them left. Before they went to war, God cut the number from ten thousand to three hundred. With three hundred fearless men, Gideon was able to win a great battle.

Don't let the size of the problem frighten you. There is no enemy greater than your Father's capabilities. It doesn't matter how big the enemy appears to be. Make yourself take your eyes off the problem and put them on the solution...God's Word. Remember, the longer you look at the problem, the more it will affect your heart. Jeremiah said, *Mine eye affecteth mine heart....* (Lamentations 3:51)

METHOD NUMBER THREE - SATAN WILL REMIND YOU OF PAST FAILURES - YOURS AND OTHERS.

You need to take heed to what you hear. Do not listen to other people's testimonies of failures. I am very careful about who I listen to. You must be careful, because out of your heart flows the forces of your life. (Proverbs 4:23)

Those forces can be good or bad. Whatever type of force comes out will determine the quality of your life and leadership. I will not listen to people tell how they believe God made them sick, or destroyed their business to get their attention, or to teach them something. Do not allow those seeds to be planted in your heart, because they will come up again, and always at the wrong time—when you least need to hear them the least!

When you first start walking by faith, there is a good possibility that you will experience failures. I did. Satan will try to hold those past mistakes over you like a threatening storm that is going to rain on your parade. The Bible says that God shall deliver you from the shame of

The Origins Of Fear

your youth. All of us were young in the Lord at one time, and did not know a lot of things. We tried to get ahead of ourselves in our faith and fell down. Get up. Clean yourself off and keep on walking. You are going to make it in a grand and glorious style, winning every victory, pasing every trial!

METHOD NUMBER FOUR - SATAN WILL CONDEMN YOU FOR NOT STUDYING ENOUGH, NOT PRAYING ENOUGH, NOT FASTING ENOUGH, NOT GOING TO CHURCH ENOUGH.

To put it simply, he will take whatever foothold you will give him. He will try to get on your back and condemn you. The definition of the word "condemnation" is "to give judgment against, to pass sentence upon, and to follow with punishment." (W.E. Vine)

There is therefore now no condemnation to them which are in Christ Jesus, who walk not after the flesh, but after the Spirit. (Romans 8:1)

There is no judgment against you, no sentence passed upon you, and no punishment following you. Satan does not have the right to punish you. He is not your God.

If you have not been doing the things you know you should have been doing, then repent. The word "repent" means "to turn from sin and turn towards God." It does not mean only to turn from sin. You have not repented until you have turned from sin **and** you have turned towards God.

The literal definition means "to change your mind and go another direction." The devil does not have the right to come in and do anything to you. If I leave my watch or billfold on the front seat of my car and the car doors are unlocked—that does not give someone the right to steal them.

Satan is called the thief because that is what he is. Satan has come to steal from you. I don't care what you have done wrong, he is not your God. Repent, confess it and ask God to forgive you. Walk away from it and forget about punishment.

Chapter III

THE FRUITS OF FEAR

In Genesis three we discovered that fear came into the human race at the fall of Adam and Eve. The sin that Adam and Eve committed was the sin of high treason. They willingly, purposefully, knowledgeably turned their backs on God and went in another direction. They gave their allegiance to another spiritual being.

When they did, they died. God had said, the day they became partakers of the knowledge of good and evil, they would die.

We know they did not die physically, but they died spiritually. And at the very moment the transgression occurred, God set out to bring about redemption.

8 And they heard the voice of the LORD God walking in the garden in the cool of the day: and Adam and his wife hid themselves from the presence of the LORD God amongst the trees of the garden.

9 And the LORD God called unto Adam, and said unto him, Where art thou?

10 And he said, I heard thy voice in the garden, and I was afraid, because I was naked (or disarmed); and I hid myself. (Genesis 3:8-10)

Fear is a spiritual force that comes from a man's heart. It is not an emotion, but it will give you emotions. Fear is not a feeling, but it will give you feelings. If you have fear in your heart, God's Word will not work in your life. Fear will short-circuit your faith. It will cause your faith to not work. If there is fear in your heart while you are saying the right things out of your mouth, the Word will not work in your life.

But if you will purpose to not move in fear in a given situation, if you will back away from fear, if you will not move in fear, you will automatically move in faith.

Why?

Because it's the only other way to go. You cannot reason with fear. But, praise God, you can live above it, and you can overcome it.

Sickness is one fruit that fear will produce in a person's life. Fear in your spirit will make your body sick.

A merry heart doeth good like a medicine: but a broken spirit drieth the bones. (Proverbs 17:22)

Medical science has proved that many things relating to the health of our bodies occurs within our bones. All

The Fruits Of Fear

kinds of diseases begin there. Solomon said, if fear is allowed to remain in a man's spirit, that fear will actually begin to affect his physical well-being, and dry his bones. We know that fear will make you sick.

The Bible says to live a carefree life, but the Bible does not say to be careless. Worry does not change anything. If you are going to do anything with your time, use it to believe God. Don't sit around worrying. Worry will not make anything better—but it will make things worse.

Jesus said in Matthew 6:34, *Take therefore no thought for the morrow....Sufficient unto the day is the evil thereof.*

You cannot do anything about the past. But you can definitely do something about the present and the future.

Fear will go forth into the kingdom of darkness to lay hold upon those things that you are afraid of. Fear will bring them to you and make them a reality in your life, just as faith will go forth into the kingdom of God and do the same thing.

Fear is a spiritual force. It has the ability to give substance to things. Just as faith is the substance of things not seen, fear can be the substance of things not seen. Job said the things which he so greatly feared came upon him. Fear is a spiritual force.

Failure is another fruit produced by fear. In Deuteronomy twenty, God gave the nation of Israel the rules they were to observe when they went to war. They are still good for us to observe today, for the principles are still true.

Whether or not you realize it, you are in a war. Whether or not you like it, you are in a war.

Many pastors in America are having a hard time getting their congregations to suit up for the war. They are running around wanting to put on their rapture clothes. They are awaiting the great escape. But while they are waiting, many of them are of no earthly good.

And the officers shall speak further unto the people, and they shall say, What man is there that is fearful and faint-hearted? let him go and return unto his house, lest his brethren's heart faint as well as his heart. (Deuteronomy 20:8)

In this scripture, God told everyone who was going to war to stay home if they were afraid.

Why?

Because fear will produce failure. If you are going to be put into a leadership capacity with people working under you, remember this fact.

Another fruit that fear produces is named in Proverbs 29:25.

Fear will put you in bondage. *The fear of man bringeth a snare....* You can read this scripture in two ways. First, the fear that is in your heart will bring a snare, or second, that your fear of other men will bring a snare.

Fear of any kind in your heart will put you in bondage to the thing you are afraid of. To be a leader, you cannot be afraid of people. That fear will put you in bondage to them. You will not be able to lead them as you should, because fear will hold you back. Remember, if you do not lead, others cannot follow.

There is no fear in love; but perfect love casteth out fear: because fear hath torment. He that feareth is not made perfect in love. (1st John 4:18)

Torment is a fruit of fear. Fear brings torment. The devil would love to kill you, but if he can't kill you, he will torment you.

Have you ever been tormented by fear? I believe Satan enjoys tormenting God's children with threats of possible harm, and with thoughts of things going wrong. I know this is especially true among God's leaders. Don't tolerate torment. God loves you and cares for you, and He is going to put you over the top!

The last fruit of fear is death. Fear can and will produce death.

In Luke twenty-one, Jesus tells of the signs that will precede His second coming.

25 And there shall be signs in the sun, and in the moon, and in the stars; and upon the earth distress of nations, with perplexity; the sea and the waves roaring;

26 Men's hearts failing them for fear.... (Luke 21:25-26)

People are dying today from heart attacks because of fear of what is happening on the earth. They see no solutions to life's problems. Fear eventually grips their minds, and then their hearts. Fear is a killer. Fear is not something to be played with, or used to manipulate people.

Chapter IV

HOW TO OVERCOME FEAR WHEN YOU REALIZE IT IS PRESENT WITH YOU

In order to overcome fear, you must first know that fear does not have dominion over you. Before you can live a fearless life and be a fearless leader, you must get the fear out of your heart.

This chapter will show you how to get the fear out and get the faith in!

Fear does not have the right to have dominion over you. It does not have the right to control your life. You must be convinced of that from the authority of God's Word. The only way you are going to become convinced is by meditating on it and confessing it to yourself.

For God hath not given us the spirit of fear; but of power, and of love, and of a sound mind.
(2nd Timothy 1:7)

Leadership: You Can Have What It Takes

This verse proves that fear does not have the right to be in our lives, because God has not given it to us. If God had given it to us, then we would have been stuck with it. But God did not give it to us. Since He didn't give it to us, we don't have to have it.

I want to share several Bible truths that you can use to get fear out of your heart, when you realize it is present with you. After you overcome fear, you can live above it. You can live in divine fearlessness.

Meditate on these spiritual weapons and practice them in your life. As you grow in the knowledge of them, you will learn how to use them whenever fear attacks you. At times, you may want to simply go down the list and check yourself by them. At other times, you may simply choose to use one method to overcome the fear. Do whatever witnesses with your heart at the time.

Number One - Fear is overcome in your life by knowing the truth.

Fear feeds on misinformation. Fear feeds on half-truths. Fear feeds, breeds, and multiplies on lies. Jesus said in John 8:32, *And ye shall know the truth, and the truth shall make you free.*

You will not have to set yourself free—the truth will set you free. The truth will set you free, when you know it.

How do you know the truth?

It is the spirit that quickeneth; the flesh profiteth nothing: the words that I speak unto you, they are spirit, and they are life. (John 6:63)

Jesus said in John seventeen, "Father, Your Word is truth." His Word is **the** truth. All truth comes from God.

What constitutes knowing the truth? Is it just having scripture memorized?

No. You can memorize scripture until you can quote the whole Bible, and still lack the truth.

When I lived in Fort Worth, I once saw a ten minute segment on television about a man who worked in a carnival. And to this day I have never seen another feat like his. He had committed to memory the entire Bible, both the Old and New Testaments. He would bet you $100 to $1 that you could not ask him a scripture which he could not quote—any scripture.

Fort Worth has several seminaries, and when this young man gave that challenge, many came for a chance. They asked him tough scriptures, not John 3:16 or Philippians 4:19. I mean those heavy-duty scriptures back in Numbers and Leviticus, where most of your pages are still stuck together.

They would say, "Leviticus 16:32," and he would immediately quote it word for word. Sometimes they would try to trick him by giving him a scripture that didn't exist. He would look at them and tell them that scripture did not exist, and take their dollar. He quoted them word for word from the King James Version.

It was simply astounding. And the evening I saw him, he had his arm in a cast, he was sick, his wife had left him, and he was broke.

Did he know the truth?

No!

How do you know someone? You know someone by having interaction with them. I know my wife because we

Leadership: You Can Have What It Takes

do things together. You know someone when you have interaction with them.

I know God will heal me.

Why?

Because I know God. I have come to know God through His Word. God has never come to me in my bedroom. He has never appeared to me. I don't need Him to appear to me. Jesus said, *Blessed are they that have not seen, and yet have believed.* (John 20:29)

If you are looking for visions, you will get some. Satan is the god of this world, and he will give you visions. He will come and visit you at night. The Bible says he will appear as an angel of light. He will give you some far-out, crazy stuff.

Remember, dreams and visions and prophecies are subject to the Word; The Word is not subject to them. What God says about you is the truth, regardless of what the circumstances say.

Believe the truth. In your churches and in your congregations, in your vision that God gives you, believe the truth. Don't believe all that others tell you. Don't believe what your head tells you. Believe what God's Word says about the anointing of God in your life.

Many times, you will have to believe the truth, contrary to what you see with your eyes. God did not say that the faith of God operates on calling those things that **are** as if they **were not**. He says it operates on calling those things that **be not** as though they **were**. (Romans 4:17)

Number two - Fear is overcome by putting your trust and your confidence in God.

Needs do not move God. Faith moves God.

25 Be not afraid of sudden fear, neither of the desolation of the wicked, when it cometh.

26 For the Lord shall be thy confidence....
(Proverbs 3:25-26)

I have my confidence in the Lord. Where do you put your confidence? This is something you do as an act of your will.

When you realize that fear has come at you, make sure your confidence and trust is in the Lord. Don't let your confidence and trust slip into the wrong things.

This is easy to let happen, particularly as the pressure mounts, or when you begin to enjoy a level of success in your life. If you are not careful, you will begin to trust and have confidence in other things, or people, or your abilities.

Number three - Fear is overcome by praising God correctly.

Praise, thanksgiving and worship—most people think of them as being the same. But they are not. Two of them are primarily for you, and one is primarily for the Lord.

Jesus said in John four that the Father seeks those who will worship Him in spirit and in truth. With all of the creative abilities of God, the one thing He cannot create, which only you can give Him, is **worship**.

God does not need your praise or thanksgiving. Yes, they do bless Him. But God does not need them.

The Lord told me once that thanksgiving is the track upon which faith carries its mighty load. You are to let your requests be made known unto God with thanksgiving. (Philippians 4:6)

Your faith is carried on the track of thanksgiving. God does not need to hear you give thanks for something you believed you received—**you** need to hear it. He doesn't doubt you have it. The devil is not telling Him you are not going to get it. Satan is telling you. And thanksgiving encourages you and keeps your faith on the line, producing.

Of the three—praise, thanksgiving, and worship, **praise** has been given to you as a spiritual weapon to use against the onslaught of the enemy.

Many people think praise was given to the body of Christ because God **needs** us to bolster Him. But that is not the case.

Praise is wonderful. The biggest book in the Bible is the Book of Praises—the book of Psalms.

1 O LORD our Lord, how excellent is thy name in all the earth! who hast set thy glory above the heavens.

2 Out of the mouth of babes and sucklings hast thou ordained strength because of thine enemies.... (Psalm 8:1-2)

Jesus, quoting this verse in Matthew 21:16, replaced the word "strength" with the word "praise." If Jesus did it, we can do it. He gave us spiritual license to do it. This was not a major change in the text.

In Hebrew, the word "praise" and the word "strength" found in this scripture come from the same root word, which means "to strengthen yourself inwardly." Praise strengthens you inwardly.

Verse 2 says, *hast thou ordained strength* (praise). So God ordained (founded, settled, and established) praise.

Why?

Because of thine enemies...."

Whose enemies?

The Lord's enemies. And are His enemies and our enemies the same enemies?

Yes! The Psalmist said the Lord ordained praise because of your enemies.

Why?

So that you might still the enemy and the avenger. Psalm 22:3 says God inhabits the praises of His people. As we begin to praise correctly, God inhabits those praises. He inhabits them to still the enemy and to quiet the avenger. God has ordained praise as a spiritual weapon.

When fear comes against you, begin to praise God correctly, according to His Word. As you praise God according to His Word, God will inhabit that praise. He will still the enemy and quiet the avenger. The fear will be turned back and will fall at God's presence.

We see this in operation in Psalm nine.

1 I will praise thee, O LORD, with my whole heart; I will shew forth all thy marvellous works.

2 I will be glad and rejoice in thee: I will sing praise to thy name, O thou most High. (Psalm 9:1-2)

What is he doing?

He is praising God.

What happens when you praise God?

God inhabits the praise.

And why is praise ordained?

To still the enemy and to quiet the avenger.

When mine enemies are turned back, they shall fall and perish at thy presence. (v.3)

How did his enemies get in God's presence?

God inhabits the praise of His people. The Psalmist did this purposely. When you read these things, realize that these men's actions were calculated to achieve a desired result, just as you act upon the Word of God to achieve a desired result.

So often, Christians read the Bible as though it were a fairy tale. The men who wrote these words were real men who faced real problems and used God's Word to overcome those problems.

The weapon of praise is one of the greatest weapons a leader has against the enemy! Many people think the book of Psalms was written just by chance, but the writers knew exactly what they were doing.

One of the literal Hebrew definitions of the word "praise" means "to praise God with open extended hands." You don't have to say one word to praise God in this manner. Simply put your hands up in the air and open them.

The devil has fought to get this knowledge out of churches all around the world. The devil hates the power of praise. He has fought for years to keep praise out of the church because he is turned back at God's presence. He is stopped right in his tracks when people begin to correctly praise God.

Do you remember Moses on the mountain looking down to the valley and seeing Joshua losing the battle? What did he do?

Moses put up his hands in praise to the Lord. As long as his hands were up, Joshua won. When his arms got tired and he put them down, the battle went the other way.

Two Israelite men were watching nearby. They understood the literal definition of the word "praise"— they watched Moses, and they watched Joshua. Soon they each got under one of his arms and they held up Moses' arms. As long as they kept his arms up, God inhabited the praise of His people, and eventually Joshua won the battle.

Why?

When God inhabits the praise of His people, the enemy is turned back and perishes at His presence.

In Acts 16:9, Paul describes a vision. He saw a man in Macedonia asking them to come and preach to them. They went and had a great revival. The devil came in. That was the thorn in Paul's flesh—a demonic spirit sent to buffet him. (2nd Corinthians 12:7)

His thorn in the flesh was not sickness and disease. It was a demon spirit that followed him around. All you have to do to verify this scripture is to read the book of Acts. The demon spirit infuriated the people. They beat Paul and Silas and threw them in prison. The Bible says they were in the innermost part of the prison, on the third level. They had their hands and legs in stocks and chains, and their backs were bleeding. The Bible says they began to praise God. They began to praise God purposely to obtain a desired result. They began to praise God in the midst of that situation, knowing that God would inhabit their praise, still the enemy, and quiet the avenger. The Bible says, as they began to praise God, the Spirit of God shook that entire prison. Their chains fell off, as did the chains of all the men in the prison, and all the prison doors opened.

The Lord told me that if our church—and the other churches—would praise Him correctly, we could obtain the same results. He would inhabit those praises and move through the congregations. People with bonds of drug addiction, alcoholism, strife, fear would be set free. He would break the chains, just as He broke the chains in that prison.

For many years, this knowledge has been lost in the church. But we are learning again.

You can praise God by yourself. You don't have to be in church. It is one of the greatest weapons you will ever find.

Number four - Fear is overcome in your life by an act of your will.

Know ye not, that to whom ye yield yourselves servants to obey, his servants ye are to whom ye obey; whether of sin unto death, or of obedience unto righteousness? (Romans 6:16)

You can by an act of your will refuse to move in fear. By an act of your sovereign will, you can refuse to be afraid. The Bible says that God has set before us life and death, blessing and cursing—and we are to choose life. You can decide to refuse to yield to fear.

Number five - Fear is overcome by confessing God's Word.

Proverbs 18:21 says that life and death is in the power of the tongue. The power of words has been working in your life from the day you learned how to talk—from the time you understood how to use your words and speak them forth. And it continues to work in your life, whether or not you read Proverbs 18:21. It is a spiritual law. God, in His infinite mercy, has given us insight into this law so we can live in harmony with it, instead of living against it. But we are living with it—one way or the other.

You can use the power of your words to overcome fear. You can get fear out of your heart and prevent it from getting hold of you by speaking God's Word out of your mouth.

Psalm 17:4 says, *Concerning the works of men* (the lives of men) *by the word of thy lips I have kept me from the paths of the destroyer.* Tie that together with Romans 10:9; *That if thou shalt confess with thy mouth the Lord Jesus, and shalt believe in thy heart that God hath raised him from the dead, thou shalt be saved.*

The word "saved" is the Greek word "sozo," which means more than just being born again. Sozo means complete salvation, wholeness of spirit, soul, and body.

Romans ten continues;

For with the heart man believeth unto righteousness; and with the mouth confession is made unto salvation. (Romans 10:10)

With your mouth, you confess yourself unto salvation. No confession equals no salvation.

You can speak God's Word and overcome fear by talking to it—talk to the fear, and talk to yourself.

When fear gets hold of you, what has left you?

Faith. And how does faith come?

Faith comes by hearing the Word of God. (Romans 10:17) "Word" in Romans 10:17 is the Greek word "rhema," which means "the spoken word." You can get faith by hearing others speak the Word to you, but you can also get faith by hearing yourself.

Jesus said in Mark 11:22, "Have the God kind of faith," or "You can use God's faith."

In verse 23, He explains how the faith of God works. He said, *For verily I say unto you, That whosoever shall say unto this mountain....*

What kind of mountain is He talking about?

The mountain is anything standing between you and the fulfillment of God's promises in your life. *...That whosoever shall say unto this mountain, Be thou removed, and be thou cast into the sea....* He is calling things that be not as though they were. He is calling the mountain in the sea. *...Be thou removed, and be thou cast into the sea; and shall not doubt in his heart, but shall believe that those things which he saith shall come to pass; he shall have whatsoever he saith.*

I want to ask you a question: have you ever confessed God's Word, and when you said it, you knew you didn't believe it in your heart?

I have. Jesus said that you cannot doubt in your heart. The devil will tell you, "It's not doing you any good walking around your room confessing the Word of God."

Would you like to find out how you go from saying it and **not believing it** to saying it and **believing it**?

Keep on saying it and saying it and saying it and saying it.

Why?

Because *faith cometh by hearing, and hearing by the word of God.* (Romans 10:17) Just keep on saying it, because one day you will be walking around confessing God's Word, and suddenly, it will energize in your spirit. That faith will come alive in your heart. Then you will say it again, and all of hell will run away from you, because the faith of God coming out of your heart through your words will lay hold upon those things you are talking about.

Faith does not come by praying. Faith does not come by seeing miracles. Miracles do not produce faith. They produce wonder and amazement. Miracles do not get people saved. The Word gets people saved. You were born again by the incorruptible seed, which is the Word of God. (1st Peter 1:23) The only way you will build the reality of redemption into your heart is by speaking forth what God has already said about you in His Word. In order to get the Word built down into your heart like a rock, you must speak it.

The word "meditate" in the Hebrew text means "to mutter, to speak to yourself in a low tone of voice." In the Greek text, it means "to revolve in your mind."

You must put God's Word into your heart. What you hear is what you will become. What you spend your time looking at is what you will trust in when the pressure comes. Take these truths and put them into your life. Start operating on them, and fear will get rooted out.

For God hath not given us the spirit of fear; but of power, and of love, and of a sound mind. (2nd Timothy 1:7)

We know from this scripture that it is your God-given scriptural right to live a life free from fear, full of power, full of love, and with a sound mind. You have a right to these things. God has not given you the spirit of fear. If God has not given it to you, then you don't have to have it. Those three things—love, power, and a sound mind—will drive out fear.

Number six - Love perfected in your life will cast out and drive out fear. (1st John 4:18)

We are supposed to walk in love as God walks in love. (Ephesians 5:2) If He says we are supposed to do it, then we are capable of doing it. God will never command or instruct you to do something you are not able to do. If He says to do it, then you can do it. The ability is there through the power of His Word in your life.

You can do it. By the operation of the Holy Spirit moving upon the Word of God that is in your heart and in your mind, you can do anything and everything God tells you to do. Philippians 4:13 says you can *do all things through Christ which strengtheneth* you. Jesus said all things are possible to him that believeth.

Paul said to walk in love. You find all types of Christians who try to walk in love. Many of them get frustrated because they don't know how to walk in love. They know they should, but they don't know how.

How do you learn to walk in love?

The number one way for you to learn to walk in love toward me is for you to first walk in the love of God toward yourself. Before you will have God's love flowing from you toward me, you have to experience God's love to you.

Why is that?

Before you can take that which God wants you to use, you must experience it yourself. Before you walk in God's love toward me, you must be experiencing God's love for you. How can you ever forgive me, until you know God has forgiven you? When you have experienced God's forgiveness for yourself, you will find it much easier to love me.

Many Christians have never become established or perfected in love. I have found that most Christians are more comfortable in a relationship with God that is based on judgment, rather than one based on forgiveness. They can better understand judgment. They can more easily understand God punishing them than they can understand Him forgiving them.

I'm not saying that God will not correct you, because Hebrews twelve says, whom God loves, He will chasten. But be sure of this: God does not use cancer, arthritis, sickness and disease, tests and trials to teach you something.

The method through which God perfects the church is exactly as Jesus said in John 15:2,3. Jesus said that every branch in Him that bears fruit, the husbandman purges. Verse 3 says,

> *Now ye are clean through the word which I have spoken unto you.* (John 15:3)

In the Greek text, the words "purge" and "clean" are exactly the same Greek word. We are clean and purged through the Word which He speaks unto us.

Ephesians 4:11-12 says He set the apostles, prophets, evangelists, pastors, and teachers in the church to perfect the saints. God always operates through His Word. Take the promises of God and meditate on them. Purpose to believe them. Then build them down into your heart by confessing the Word of God.

Chapter V

BECOMING A FEARLESS LEADER

We are going to examine what I like to call divine fearlessness. People want their leaders to be fearless.

Jesus is our ultimate example as a leader. I believe the word "fearless" best describes His ministry. He never reacted in fear to anything that came against Him. And He was faced with several opportunities that we could classify as terrifying.

Jesus was fearless, and we can become like Him. As a matter of fact, it is our destiny to be exactly like him—see Romans 8:29!

In this chapter you are going to find statements of fact about you, taken directly from scripture. Meditate on these truths, and purpose in your heart to believe them. Build them down into your heart. As you do, they will build into you a fearless attitude—a fearlessness consciousness that will lead you to new heights in your walk with God!

Fact number one - You do not have to be afraid, because God is your protection and your strength. (Psalm 46:1)

Quit reading the book of Psalms as if these were just pretty songs that these men made up. These songs came out of their hearts when they were facing real problems and real circumstances just like you are facing. God moved upon them by the Holy Ghost, and they sang forth these songs.

These psalms were statements of their faith—their confidence, their trust in God. They became strong on purpose, just as you must become strong on purpose.

God is our refuge (or our protection) *and strength, a very present help in trouble.* (Psalm 46:1)

Where is God when trouble comes?

Very present.

And what is He very present to do?

Help. When trouble comes to the front door, God does not go out the back door.

Therefore will not we fear.... The word "therefore" means "because of this."

Because of what?

Because God is our refuge (and our protection) and strength,

2 Therefore will not we fear, though the earth be removed, and though the mountains be carried into the midst of the sea;

3 Though the waters thereof roar and be troubled, though the mountains shake with the swelling thereof. Selah. (Psalm 46:2-3)

He said, "I will not be afraid." Don't you like it when people talk like that? Don't you like it when those words come out of someone's mouth?

This was a statement of fact in his life. And you can have the same things, if you will build them down into your heart. You must realize, recognize, believe, and receive into your heart that God is your protection and your strength.

God did not promise to be; He **is!** God **is** your protection and strength. David said, "though the earth be removed, I will not be afraid."

You do not become like that overnight. You build the reality of this down into your heart on purpose, as an act of your will. You purpose to believe. You purpose to have that attitude.

You build it into yourself by spending time in the Word of God, by spending time in prayer, by confessing God's Word, letting it develop on the inside. You build it into yourself by facing fearful situations and circumstances, and running this through your mind: "God is my protection; God is my strength."

You build this into yourself, line upon line, precept upon precept, just as a man builds a brick wall. You build this knowledge into your spirit. Then one day you get into a troubled situation. You look at it and realize that deep within you there is no panic, but rather confidence. There is peace, ability, and power. You look at the situation, knowing that, with God's help, you will change these events for the better.

You will have a whole different attitude. Instead of running around like a chicken with its head cut off, you rise up in the power and ability of that which is already birthed in you by the Holy Ghost.

1 The LORD is my light and my salvation; whom shall I fear? the LORD is the strength of my life; of whom shall I be afraid?

2 When the wicked, even mine enemies and my foes, came upon me to eat up my flesh, they stumbled and fell.

3 Though an host should encamp against me, my heart shall not fear: though war should rise against me, in this will I be confident. (Psalm 27:1-3)

Be confident of what?

He was confident that the Lord was his light, his salvation, and his strength. He did not have to be afraid.

You do not have to be afraid, either, because the Lord **is** your light, your salvation, and your strength!

Fact number two - You do not have to be afraid, for God is your help.

10 Fear thou not; for I am with thee: be not dismayed; for I am thy God: I will strengthen thee; yea, I will help thee; yea, I will uphold thee with the right hand of my righteousness. (Isaiah 41:10)

Who or what is the right hand of God's righteousness? Jesus.

What did He say He was going to uphold you with?

The right hand of His righteousness, Who is Jesus. Our lives are being upheld by the Lord Himself. For us to go under, He would have to go under. And that is not going to happen.

11 Behold, all they that were incensed against thee shall be ashamed and confounded: they shall be as nothing; and they that strive with thee shall perish.

12 Thou shalt seek them, and shalt not find them, even them that contended with thee: they that war against thee shall be as nothing, and as a thing of nought. (Isaiah 41:11-12)

That is an attitude which is missing in the body of Christ today. I am not saying that we should act like spiritual bullies, but we do need to start believing these scriptures. A lot of foolishness happens in the world today against the body of Christ which has no right to be happening. But it will keep on happening as long as we keep letting it go on.

God said, they that stand against us will pass away. It's time for the body of Christ to quit apologizing for what we believe. It's time for us to quit being intimidated by the threats of the world. This is the greatest hour the church has ever had to shine forth and be everything God has made us to be. We must not let this opportunity slip through our fingers.

The Lord will confound our enemies, and their effect upon us will be nothing. But it all begins with our believing scriptures like these, and by our no longer passing off harassment as persecution.

I know persecution will come, but God said, they that contend with us will be as nothing.

13 For I the LORD thy God will hold thy right hand, saying unto thee, Fear not; I will help thee. (Isaiah 41:13)

How much more personal can He get? It's as if He is reaching down, taking your right hand, and saying, "Don't be afraid; I will help you."

What will it take to get it across to us that God will help us? He said, "I'm holding your right hand. Quit being scared; I'm here to help you."

God wants us to rise up and face fear. But many of us are saying, "I want to leave. I want to leave." He is holding our hand, trying to pull us back, and we are trying to go the other way. He said, "Don't be afraid!"

In order to be a leader, you must get your thinking right. Start thinking as God thinks, because your brain was "wired" by God to think His way. When you start thinking His way, your brain will function at a higher level than ever before. Proverbs 10:7 says the memory of the just is blessed.

There are little things you can do to help your memory. Your brain just gets lazy. For example, when you look in the telephone directory for a phone number, once you find the number and begin dialing, don't keep looking back at the number in the book each time you dial only two digits. Train yourself to remember the whole number. I know that sounds like a small thing, but you will be amazed by how much training yourself in little things will help you in big things.

Fact number three - You do not have to be afraid, for God will deliver you.

I sought the LORD, and he heard me, and delivered me from all my fears. (Psalm 34:4)

What will the Lord deliver you from?

All your fears.

When?

When you seek Him.

17 The righteous cry, and the LORD heareth, and delivereth them out of all their troubles. (Psalm 34:17)

Who are the righteous?

We are the righteous.

The righteous cry, and what happens?

The Lord hears and delivers them out of all their troubles. Why should you be afraid, when the Lord **will** deliver you out of all your troubles. He will deliver you—not maybe, not hope so, not might. **He will!**

Fact number four - You do not have to be afraid, for the Lord HAS GIVEN YOU the victory.

You can lead fearlessly, for the Lord has given you the victory. Notice in Joshua eight. *And the LORD said unto Joshua Fear not, neither be thou dismayed: take all the people of war with thee...* (Joshua 8:1)

We learned from Deuteronomy 20:8 that "all the people of war" were all the people who were not afraid.

...and arise, go up to Ai: see, I have given into thy hand the king of Ai, and his people, and his city, and his land. (Joshua 8:1)

It is important for us to note that Joshua is not at Ai yet. He has not gone there yet. He has not pulled one sword out of its sheath. And God tells Joshua here to get up and go to Ai, because He has given the city to him.

How can God tell Joshua that He has given him the city when Joshua wasn't even at the city?

Because God calls those things which be not as though they were. (Romans 4:17) God speaks of the end from the beginning. (Isaiah 46:10)

Why does God speak of the end from the beginning; and why does God call things which be not as though they were?

Because that is how He gets them to become something different. That is called faith. Some people would say, if you say you are healed when they can plainly see that you are not, you are lying. But notice, God told Joshua to go to Ai, because He had given him the city.

Was God lying?

Of course not!

What was God doing?

He was saying what He believed and knew to be true, even though what he said was contrary to earthly circumstances. **We have been instructed to do the same thing.**

Second Corinthians 4:13 shows us the two components of faith; the two things that make up faith. It says because we believe, we speak. Faith is made up of two things—believing and speaking.

This is even clearer in Mark 11:23. Jesus said, *Whosoever shall say unto this mountain... and shall not doubt in his heart, but shall believe....*

God told Joshua to rise up and go down to the city, because He had already given it to him. God called that which was not as though it were.

Whosoever believeth that Jesus is the Christ is born of God.... (1st John 5:1) Are you a "whosoever who believes Jesus is the Christ?" Then you are born of God!

Now look at what verse four says about you.

For whatsoever (this is you!) is born of God overcometh the world: and this is the victory that overcometh the world, even our faith. (1st John 5:4)

You do not have to be afraid. God has given you the victory. And that victory is in the form of His faith which He imparted to your spirit when you were born again. When you hear the Word of God, faith comes; the ability to believe God comes. The ability to believe and speak the faith in your heart gives you the ability to overcome the world. You have the victory inside of you. You do not have to go looking for it; you are carrying it around with you all the time. The victory is already in your heart. You need only to get it out. The victory is in you.

Before God gave you faith, that faith was His faith. Now you have His faith that He put in you. And before He gave it to you, He tested it, He tried it, He proved it.

God does not need to test your faith. He already tested it. If he doesn't know what this faith is going to do, then who does know?

Where did God prove it? Where did He put it to the test?

He tested it and proved it when He used that faith to raise Jesus from the dead! Praise God, it worked! Jesus arose from the grave after three days. But not stopping there, He went right on to Heaven and sat down at the right hand of God.

Paul prayed, in Ephesians 1:19-23, that we know the power of God—the same power that God used to raise His Son. For that same power has been given unto you. That's the same power that God generated in this earth to raise His Son from the clutches of death and to bring Him out of that horrible pit and set Him at His own right hand. That same power that He proved could overcome the world is in you now!

That very power flowed from Peter, James, and John, their shadows falling upon the sick and healing them. These men were not embalmed with religious tradition. They shook off the shackles of tradition and walked out into the new light of God's Word. They simply believed what Jesus said. The didn't try to figure out why it would not work; they figured out why it would work. God help us to come to that same point.

Fact number five - You do not have to be afraid, for God delights in giving you the kingdom.

31 But rather seek ye the kingdom of God; and all these things shall be added unto you.

32 Fear not, little flock.... (Luke 12:31-32)

There is not a more helpless animal on the earth than a sheep. Sheep have no weapons to defend themselves. They run slowly. Their feet have no claws. Their teeth are only for chewing, not biting.

*Fear not, little flock; for it is your Father's **good** pleasure to give you the kingdom.* (Luke 12:32)

God delights in giving you the kingdom. I cannot express in words what this scripture means to me. I find peace in knowing that God delights and finds pleasure in giving me the kingdom.

Psalm 35:27 says God takes pleasure in the prosperity of His servants. The Bible says God is withholding no good thing from them who walk uprightly. He wants you to be blessed. God is not against your having money—He is against money having you. He would much more desire for you to have money, than some sinner.

Fact number six - You do not have to be afraid, because God is for you, God is with you, and God is in you.

5 I called upon the LORD in distress: the LORD answered me, and set me in a large place.

6 The LORD is on my side; I will not fear: what can man do unto me?

7 The LORD taketh my part with them that help me: therefore shall I see my desire upon them that hate me.

8 It is better to trust in the LORD than to put confidence in man. (Psalm 118:5-8)

The Hebrew text in verse six says, "The Lord is for me." Paul, quoting this in Romans 8:31, said, ...*If God be for us* (and He is), *who can be against us?* One translation reads, *If God be for us, no one can succeed as our enemy.* You do not have to be afraid, because God is for you. He told me once that teams have been chosen, and He was on my side.

Jesus said, when the Spirit of truth comes, He would never leave us nor forsake us, even unto the ends of the earth. God is with you.

...Greater is he that is in you, than he that is in the world. (1st John 4:4) Greater is He that is in you than every poverty spirit that would come against you. Greater is He that is in you than every sickness and disease that would attack you. Greater is He that is in you than every kind of oppression, depression, recession, or inflation that would try to come against you. The greater One lives in you. Greater is He that is in you than he that is in the world. You do not have to be afraid, for the greater One lives in you. There is no reason to be afraid, for He that is in you is greater than fear!

Fact number seven - You do not have to be afraid, for trouble does not separate you from God.

35 Who shall separate us from the love of Christ? shall tribulation, or distress, or persecution, or famine, or nakedness, or peril, or sword?

36 As is it written, For thy sake we are killed all the day long; we are accounted as sheep for the slaughter. (Romans 8:35-36)

Did He say that's the way it is?

No. He is not making a statement, but asking a question: "Are we sheep sent to the slaughter?" The following verse answers his own question.

37 Nay, in all these things we are more than conquerors through him that loved us.

38 For I am persuaded.... (Romans 8:37-38)

You do not get **persuaded** by listening to one tape. You must build persuasion down into your heart. That is what I am giving you—I am giving you things to build with. I am handing you a load of bricks for you to build with. Build your house upon the rock, and when the storm comes, you will be high and dry. (Matthew 7:21-25) I don't care how strong the storm is, as long as it is beating on the house, and not on me.

> *38 For I am persuaded, that neither death, nor life, nor angels, nor principalities, nor powers, nor things present, nor things to come,*
>
> *39 Nor height, nor depth, nor any other creature, shall be able to separate us from the love of God, which is in Christ Jesus our Lord.* (Romans 8:38-39)

You do not have to be afraid, for trouble does not separate you from God. You can be just like the prophet Elisha in Second Kings six. The servant went out in the morning to get water, and saw that the Syrian army had encircled the whole town. He came running in saying, "Oh, master! What will become of us?"

The prophet went out and said, "Lord, open his eyes."

Suddenly, the servant's eyes were opened, and he saw surrounding them on the hills, chariots of fire with angels in them. The prophet said, *Fear not: for they that be with us are more than they that be with them.* (2nd Kings 6:16)

You have more going for you than the devil has against you. You have more working on your behalf than the devil has working against you. Nothing shall separate you from the love of God that is in Christ Jesus your Lord.

Fact number eight - you do not have to be afraid, for God is your source of supply.

If you are smart, you will make Jesus the head of your house and let Him become the bread provider. You still work. You do everything you have been doing. But turn the authority over to Him. One of the definitions of the word "Lord" in Romans ten (if any man shall confess Jesus as Lord) means **bread provider.** Confess Jesus as your bread provider.

But my God shall supply all your need according to his riches in glory by Christ Jesus. (Philippians 4:19)

God is your source of supply. Because of that fact, there is no reason to be afraid of recession, inflation, depression, or lack of any kind. You can't go under, because you are going over!

Fact number nine - You do not have to be afraid, for John 17:14,16 says you are in the world, but you are not of the world.

That means, if the world says, "you must be sick sometime," you don't have to. That means, if the world says, "you are going under," you're not. That means, if the world says, "you can't get financing," you can. That means, if the world says, "you can't be healed," you can be healed.

Why?

Because you are in the world, but you are not of it. What is of the world is of no concern to you. We are in the world, and we deal with the world, but it does not rule us. It is not the final authority. The final authority in our lives is God's Word. Make God's Word the final authority.

I get advice. I get all kinds of counsel. I seek out people who know what they are talking about. But when their advice is contrary to God's Word, I am going with the Word.

You are not going under. You are going over! The Lord has made your feet like the hind's feet. He has caused you to walk on your high places! You are blessed coming in and blessed going out; you are blessed in the city, and blessed in the field. Everything you set your hand to is blessed and caused to prosper.

When other men see you, they know that God is with you, and they are afraid of you. They will not stand in front of you to hinder you. God has blessed your storehouse, and has commanded the blessing upon you in everything you set your hand to do.

Everything you do will work for the benefit of yourself, your spouse, your children, your family, your church, your community, and your nation.

How do you get confidence like that?

By confessing it. I don't always feel up, but the world keeps on moving, whether or not I feel up for it. So I just do like David did. David said, "This is the day that the Lord has made; I will be glad and rejoice in it." He set the tone for the whole day. He let it be known in all the spiritual kingdom what his day was going to be like. He said, "This is the day which the Lord hath made. God is in control of this day in my life, and I will rejoice and be glad in it."

Leadership: You Can Have What It Takes

Jesus said that the Word is alive! (John 6:63) You have a living weapon in your hands. The Sword of the Spirit is a living weapon. It has life of its own in it. All you need to do is hang onto it. It will fight. This sword is so sharp that it will plunge into the spiritual realm. It will reach into wherever the demon forces are. It will reach into the spiritual realm and carve up the devil!

The next time the devil comes knocking on your door, don't stand there saying, "Oh! Where did I miss it? Where did I go wrong?"

Instead, take the Sword of the Spirit and attack him. If the devil cuts off the finances in your life and tries to shut you down—get mad at him!

You may need to throw a fit at the devil. The church has been retreating long enough. We have singles retreats, and married couples retreats. We need to quit having retreats and start advancing!

Jesus said for us to go forth and possess the land. Do you know who He said were the ones who take the kingdom of God?

He said the violent take it by force. Jesus said the kingdom of God suffereth, or allows, violence. And it is the violent who take it by force. There comes a time when you must fight for what belongs to you.

Sooner or later, you must stand up for your family. You must be fed up with the curse of the law hanging around your house. And when you do, you will launch an all-out attack against Satan in every area of your life. Just walk up to him, look him in the face, and say, "Devil, if you want a fight—you have it!"

Chapter VI

THE NON-COMPROMISING LEADER

Have you ever noticed the spiritual emphasis that is placed on the word "new"? God talks about the new birth, new creation, having a new covenant, having your mind renewed, singing a new song, the new Jerusalem.

He is the God of new beginnings. Tomorrow is a new day. No one has ever lived tomorrow before. No one has ever been where we are going. We are on an uncharted sea. We are going places where no one in humanity has ever been—to tomorrow; a new beginning, a new start.

We must make the most of today, so that we will be well-prepared for tomorrow. Anything we have done in the past is gone. We cannot take yesterday's victories with us into tomorrow. Every day is a new day, a new beginning. Each of us, as members of the body of Christ, need to determine that our walk with the Lord will be better and closer tomorrow than it was today.

I ask you this question: are you satisfied with the spiritual progress you are making? I ask that question because I want to see you grow. I want the rest of your life to be the best of your life.

In this chapter we will discuss a great Bible principle which will show you how to have the best out of life.

To be a leader, you must make your life be an example to others. If people do not look up to you, then they will not have anything to follow. **You cannot be a leader and live a compromising life.**

While in prayer recently, I heard the voice of God speaking through my spirit. He said, "Son, you can live without compromise."

It is possible for us to live our lives without compromise.

Know ye not that they which run in a race run all, but one receiveth the prize? So run, that ye may obtain. (1st Corinthians 9:24)

The Holy Spirit, through the apostle Paul, is telling us that life is like a race. You run this race, whether or not you want to. You cannot get off the course.

Some people say, "Well, I'm going to drop out of the race."

No, you are not. You are going to stay in the race until you go to heaven, or until you go to hell.

Many people in my generation tried to drop out of the race. The wanted to merely sit around, be taken care of, and party. If they worked, they worked only so that they could party.

Again, Paul says,

Know ye not that they which run in a race run all, but one receiveth the prize? So run, that ye may obtain. (1st Corinthians 9:24)

Some say, "We're all down here in the old rat race."

Brother, I'm not in a rat race. I am not racing rats. I am a king in Christ Jesus, and you are a king in Christ Jesus. I am valuable, and I am important. I am somebody, for I am in Christ, and He is in me. He died for me, so don't call me a rat. I'm a king! Some may run with rats, but I'm going to run with kings!

Paul says we are all involved in a race. Then he tells us how to run the race. We are to run to win the prize.

Have you watched the Olympics? Do you think any of the runners line up at the starting line thinking, "I just hope I get fifth place"? If that's their attitude, they will not win the race. There's no way they could win it; they are beaten before they even start.

When they line up, each one is thinking, "I can win this race, and I'm going to run to win!"

Paul says for us to run the race to win the prize. He said to run so that you may win. He didn't say to run to get second place, or fourth place.

Unfortunately, that type of thinking is foreign to most Christians, for we have been taught that the proper Christian attitude is to win some, lose some.

That is not what Paul said. Paul said for us to run to win the prize. To be a leader, this attitude must be developed in you.

The first thing to do is to chase mediocrity out of your life. So many people are living below their potential, because they have grown content with their lot in life—or they believe God wants them to be content with their lot in life. They have no ambition to accomplish more with their abilities. Needless to say, no one will follow someone who is going nowhere.

You can do great things in your life when you decide you are going to—and not a moment before. Decide today that every day, you will grow stronger and stronger in the Word of God. You are in a race. Since you must run, you may as well run to obtain the prize. Don't be content with merely finishing the race.

So many believers today need to have their minds renewed to this scripture which says, run to win. The body of Christ needs to grow into this knowledge. Don't resist growing up spiritually. Refuse to stay the same in your fellowship with the Lord. Run to obtain the prize. Do the things God's Word teaches. They will help you grow.

The thought of running the race to obtain the prize is so contrary to most Christian thinking. Christians have been so religiously brainwashed that many of them don't even realize they are in a race. Those certainly are not trying to obtain the prize. They are not even on the track—or so they think.

The truth of the matter is that we are in the race. We are, whether or not we want to be in the race, or think we are in the race, or like being in the race.

Many people think that after they get born again and filled with the Holy Ghost, they can drop out and take a "whatever will happen, will happen" attitude. They have been taught that the real "faith" person is the one who just takes whatever happens.

There is only one thing wrong with that: it isn't true.

Things will happen in your life (even if you are a born again, spirit-filled Christian) that the Lord doesn't have anything to do with. You did it, or the devil did it. But don't blame God, for He didn't do it.

In the Old Testament, God said, *...I have set before you life and death, blessing and cursing: therefore choose life, that both thou and thy seed may live.* (Deuteronomy 30:19) In other words, the decision is yours. Make up your mind what you will have.

You decide. But once you decide, don't blame God. You choose what you want. Peace or turmoil—you decide what you want. If you want peace, if you want health—God's Word will show you how to obtain them. If don't want them, then just keep living as you formerly lived. The choice is yours.

You can get up from reading this book and do anything you jolly well please. You can do anything you want. You are not a puppet on a string. You are a human being, and you have a sovereign will. You are made in the image and likeness of God. You can choose your own destiny. You are the only creature on this planet who has that ability. You can determine your destiny.

Paul, writing to us by the Spirit of God, says that all of us are running a race. He also says something else that is foreign to most of our previous upbringings. *...So run that ye may obtain* is so different from most of our previous religious teachings. Most of us have been taught that a good Christian is one who floats along on the waves of life, taking what comes, going whichever way the wind blows.

"**Running the race to obtain the prize?** We'll be happy if we can hold out to the end. Pray for us, brother, that we hold out to the end. We just want a little log cabin in glory land."

That type of thinking and reasoning has gotten many of us into a mess.

Paul says for us to run so that we may obtain the prize. He didn't say to run just to finish. He didn't say to just start. He didn't say to run just to get last place. **He said, run to win.**

Even as you read this book, whether you know it or not, you are also involved in a fight. The Bible calls it the good fight of faith.

Before I got turned on to Jesus, I was in a lot of fights. And I was never in a good one. Even the ones I won were not good ones. There is nothing good about someone hitting you in the face with a fist. It is not fun.

So what does Paul mean by a good fight?

The only good fight is a fight you know you will win, before you ever start. He said to fight the good fight of faith.

When I was young, I was taught, "Charles, don't ever go out looking for a fight. But if you ever get in one, do whatever you have to do to win. Pick up a stick, a board, a rock, a brick, a chair, a table, or anything. If you get in a fight, fight to win."

I'm not saying yea or nay to that, but I will say that the attitude of winning is a good attitude.

The Non-Compromising Leader

Listen to me: you are not a good loser. Humans were not made to be good losers. You can be a good sport, and you should be. But don't teach your children to be good losers. Teach them to be good winners.

Do you see the difference?

In games or in sports, you may not always win. For example, I don't play Monopoly with my wife Rochelle. In fifteen years, we have played at least 100 Monopoly games. I have won once. I don't play Monopoly anymore, because it is bad for my inner image. I like to do things that I know I will win. I'll play football or basketball with Rochelle, but I will not play Monopoly.

Jesus said,

The thief cometh not, but for to steal, and to kill, and to destroy: I am come that they might have life, and that they might have it more abundantly. (John 10:10)

The word "life" in the Greek text is the word "zoe," which literally translated, means "life like God has it." Jesus literally said, *I have come so that you might have life like God has it, so that you might live like He lives, and have the quality of life that God has.* Jesus said, *I have come to give you the life of God.*

That is the prize which is set before us. That is the mark we are moving toward. That is what we are leading others toward. That is the thing which is set before us. That is what we are setting our goals on and making our moves toward.

We are to have life: not as beggars, not as people sick sometimes—healed sometimes, broke sometimes—prosperous sometimes. We are to have life as children of God, experiencing the kind of life that Jesus came to give us; life as God has it.

Can you imagine how well God lives? Can you conceive of waking up every day knowing when your feet hit the floor that it will be a good day, because you have life as God has it? That makes living something to be excited about.

Jesus said, *I have come to give you that kind of life.* You do not have to crawl around in the mud. Don't let circumstances rule you and dictate to you, pushing you down and putting their ugly heels on your neck. Jesus said, *I have come to give you life as God has it.* That is the best kind of life!

Paul said, "If you are going to run the race, run to win the prize." We must get the previous upbringing of religious tradition, the chains of bondage, off our minds and out of our spirits. We must quit seeing ourselves as losers and start seeing ourselves as winners and leaders.

God loves you. He is for you. God is on your side. His Son came to give you life—life like He has. He did not come to break you, or bend you. He came to give you life. He came to lift you up out of the miry clay, and put your feet on the rock to stay!

God is on your side! He came to set you free, not to put you in bondage.

If God wanted you in bondage, He would have let the devil have you. Satan will grind you into powder, if he can. Satan hates you. He would just as soon kill you as look at you. I don't care if you served him diligently for forty years, he still hates you. And the reward for all that faithfulness is hell as your eternal home.

For a while, someone else's prayers can carry you—but not forever. My wife and I cannot carry our whole church. I wish that I could stand up on Sunday mornings, or Tuesday nights, or on the radio, and pray one prayer for everyone in the church, and have it meet everyone's needs. But it doesn't work that way. A time in your life will come when you will have to pray for yourself. Don't be afraid of that time, for you will discover that you could have done it months earlier.

At that time, you will step into a realm where it is you and God. That scares some people, because all of their life, mommy or daddy or someone took care of them. But someday, it is going to be you and God and the Word. So you'd better be ready. You don't have to be afraid of it, because God is just the same. The Word has the power, and He has made up for your shortcomings.

PREPARATIONS

If you are going to win the prize, you must be prepared to do three things.

Number one - You must be prepared to run.

Many Christians are not prepared to run. For some reason, they think Christianity is a sit-down, lay-down life until Jesus comes again.

Run in the race? They haven't even suited up. They are still in bed. They aren't running. They are sitting at home watching other believers run, saying, "Oh! I wish I could do that." They hear preachers on TV say, "You can do it!" and they say, "Oh, I wish that were true."

Sooner or later, you will have to believe what is being taught to you. Then you must act on it, in order to whip the devil. The devil and you are eyeball to eyeball. You are going to whip him. He will tell you that you can't, but you can, because this is the victory that has overcome the world—your faith. (1st John 5:4)

You will beat him. You will put him under your feet. You will walk on him, and it will feel so good!

Do you know why?

Because you were made to rule. You were made to live without compromise. You were made to walk in that realm of life, in that quality of life. You were made in the image and likeness of God. We have not begun to understand what that means. We have not begun to comprehend what kind of beings we are. You need to be prepared to run.

Number two - You need to be prepared to win.

Many people are not prepared to win. Much is being written today about the fear of success. Some people are afraid to succeed. They think if they accomplish their goals, or exceed their quotas, then others will begin to expect that level of success or output all the time. To keep from being put in that position, they never push themselves to their maximum effort.

Some are afraid of succeeding because they are afraid of failing. The fear of failure is so strong in them that they never try anything new, nor push themselves beyond a level they are comfortable with.

These fears can be overcome. They must be overcome. (See the chapter on overcoming fear.)

If you do not overcome fears, you will never win. If you never win, you cannot be a leader.

Many times, people who run to win are not prepared for another aspect of winning. When a person decides to break out of the pack and do more with their life, oftentimes they experience very surprising side-effects. They soon encounter negative reactions from friends, family, and co-workers. As they begin to move into a higher level of authority and productivity in life, they discover that not everyone is excited about this success. Friends begin to change in their actions toward them. Co-workers sometimes get the impression that the winner and leader thinks he is "too good for them."

If you are going to run to win, and not settle for second best, then prepare yourself for this truth: winning is not always easy. Many do not know how to treat a winner/leader. They are uncomfortable, and oftentimes they do not want to be around them. Winners/leaders are many times not prepared for this aspect of winning. Winning is wonderful, but frequently there is the unexpected price to pay: friends who no longer want to be your friends; persecution from family members, because you have broken out of the little box they put you in; ridicule from co-workers who, by your performance and attitude, have become convicted that they are not doing enough with their lives.

Number three - You need to be prepared to finish.

Many people get born again, filled with the Holy Ghost, and turned on to the things of God. They hear about the return of Jesus, and think He is going to come back next week, or next month, or next year. They begin to run the race accordingly. They are going to obtain the prize, but Jesus doesn't come back next week, next month, next year.

These people are not prepared to finish the race, and they fall by the wayside.

Have you ever watched races where a runner takes off at the sound of the gun and gets far ahead of everyone else? The broadcaster says, "Wow! They are really tearing up the track today." They get so far ahead. Then comes the last lap, and the other runners start passing by. They lead nearly the whole race, but finish last.

Do you know why?

They were not prepared to finish. The same thing can be true in your walk of faith. You must be well prepared, so you won't run out of steam when you need it the most.

Many people, after they get saved, become discouraged because they thought the Christian race was a hundred-yard dash, when it was a twenty-six-mile marathon. You must pace yourself with consistency. Do not run/lead in quick flashes of speed. Be consistent and determined. Remember, you are a long-distance runner.

Yes, Jesus may come back tomorrow, but you need to run as if He might not.

However, that statement does not give us the right to be lazy and do nothing, giving the excuse of not wanting to overextend ourselves. No. We need to be about our Father's business and be involved in the things of God. Just be careful that you don't start things that you are not prepared to finish.

This is particularly true when you are enlisting others to help you accomplish your goals. Make sure that you do not leave a trail of unfinished projects behind you. If you do, people will soon lose confidence in you and in your ability to hear the voice of God. If you are going to stand before people and tell them, "God told me to do this," be sure He told you to do it!

Let's look now at long-distance runners and running. the real mark of credibility for a leader is consistency over a period of time. Let us say that you wanted to become a marathon runner. A long-distance runner must do three things in order to accomplish his goals.

Number one, he must train. Number two, he must prepare himself. Number three, he must set his mind.

What makes you a runner? If you went out and bought a book on running, would that make you a runner?

No.

What if you bought a pair of running shoes. Would that make you a runner?

It would help, but having the right shoes does not make you a runner.

What if you ate all the right foods. Would that help you be a long-distance runner?

To a degree, that would help, but you still would not be a runner.

All three things would help you to become a runner. But what is the one thing that you must do if you are going to be a long-distance runner? You have to get out there and run!

Let's say you wanted to become a long-distance runner. You have bought books, bought good shoes, and changed your diet. Tomorrow morning you are going to begin running. Bright and early, you get up and put on your designer jogging suit, your $100 color-coordinated running shoes, your tape recorder, and here you go—look out world! You throw open the front door and start running, with isions of the New York City marathon in your head.

You feel good running from the front door to the road in front of your house. The only problem is that by the time you get to the street, you think you are going to die. Parts of your body you didn't know you had start screaming at you, "What are you doing!"

Your mind is saying, "We are working out!" Your legs are saying, "No, we are going back into the house to have a chocolate milkshake."

When people start working out, they usually become discouraged at first, because they see someone who has been working out for a longer time doing better than them. The same thing is true in Christianity.

If you want to train to run in a marathon, you start with a block. Then you get up to a mile, then two miles, then four, finally then up to twenty-six miles. Eventually, you could do it, if there was nothing physically wrong with you. If you made up your mind that you were going to do it, and you disciplined yourself, you could make it. But you are not going to do it the first day.

Some Christians we know become discouraged when they first start to run the race of faith, because, in comparing themselves to my wife and me, they fall short. They say, "Rochelle and Charles seem to get answers every time they pray. They seem to get their needs met. All these things seem to be working for them. But it doesn't seem to be working that good for me. Why?"

It's because they are still tiring out running from the house to the street. That's how far we used to run in faith. But because we kept running, now we can run around the block. And eventually you will be able to run around the block, also.

But you are not going to run around the block until you have run from the house to the street. Paul said that we grow "from faith to faith." (Romans 1:17)

Rochelle and I are using our faith today for things that we never could have tackled five years ago. It would have destroyed us, just as it would probably destroy some people to take off running for twenty-six miles.

But you can look at your life and say, "I'm going to run this race, and I'm going to obtain the prize. When Jesus comes back, He is going to give me the prize of the high calling that is in Christ Jesus. I am going to obtain the prize, and I am going to run the race!"

Don't become discouraged because someone who has been in the Word longer than you is running faster, or is ahead. Don't become discouraged, but rather be encouraged. You are now where they once were. The fact that they are no longer there should encourage you to get where they are. Do you know what will happen when you get there? They won't be there, for they are still growing and progressing—and showing you the way.

A word to the wise: don't do this because of competition or jealousy or envy. I have known people in the ministry who have tried to compete with other ministers. That kind of competition is a trap. You cannot compete with them. By the time you get where they are now, they will no longer be there. Keep your heart pure, and walk with the Lord. Eventually you can catch up to them.

I guarantee that the only way you will reach your goal is by putting one foot in front of the other. Walk by faith. Live one day at a time. That is how everyone lives—one day at a time. That is true for Rochelle, for me, for Bob Tilton, for R.W. Schambach.

Some people look up to us and say, "You are so far ahead of us."

But we too live one day at a time. We do not have some mystical, magical formula. God is not doing something behind the scenes for us, keeping us ahead. Rochelle and I have dedicated our lives, night and day, to living by faith. We are acting upon everything we have found in the Word. We have not compromised one part of the Bible. We are not compromising, and we will not compromise.

If anyone can have success, it is you. I am sure of that, because we did. All you have to do is take one step at a time.

Jesus said, do not worry about tomorrow, take care of today. Take care of what you know. Handle today and plan ahead. The Bible says that any enterprise is built on wise planning.

Plan ahead. But take care of where you are. Don't get so caught up in where you could be that you miss where you are. Prepare yourself not only to run, but also to finish; and not only to finish, but to win. Be prepared to pay the price to get to the end, and win!

Chapter VII

YOU CAN BE A LEADER

Know ye not that they which run in a race run all, but one receiveth the prize? So run, that ye may obtain. (1st Corinthians 9:24)

I want to encourage you to go out and run the race. If God said for you to run to obtain the prize, then you can obtain the prize. You can be a leader. You can be someone who affects people's lives. God does not tell you to do something that He has not equipped you to do. You can have the very best there is in your life.

I am not referring to material things only. That is a part of it. But I am talking about every area of your life— spiritually, mentally, your family, your relationship with your friends, your job, your social circles. You can have the best there is in life, if you purpose to have it.

So many people accept compromise. They accept compromise in their marriage, in their relationship with their children, in their relationship with friends, and on their job. They know they could do more, but they don't, because "that is what everybody else is doing."

You are not everybody else! You are a child of the Most High God. God has placed a higher standard for you, and you can obtain it.

I want everything in my life that Jesus had in His mind when He said, "I have come to give you life as God has it." I realize that His idea of my life is greater than my idea of my life, so I am going to get rid of mine, and replace it with His. I am going to have His image of my life, instead of my image.

This is running to obtain the prize. I want the prize. The prize is the life of God; God's life in my life.

I want to relate to you one of the greatest lies Satan has ever sold to the body of Christ. This lie stops more people from becoming a leader than any other lie I know of.

People say, "Charles, I love to come to church and hear what you say. Oh, I would love to be what you say I can be, and I would love to do the things you say I can do. But I just can't. And the reason why I can't is that I was born into the wrong family." Or, others say, "...My skin is not the right color,", or, "...I didn't have the right education." "...I was born in the wrong part of town."

You can read in Judges about Gideon. Gideon was nothing but a dirt farmer. His nation was held in bondage by another nation. He could not go anywhere without having to report to someone. Armed soldiers were all around him. His father worshipped idols.

One day while he was farming, God spoke to him and said, "Gideon, I have chosen you to deliver Israel."

God took this ignorant dirt farmer who knew nothing about the things of God and delivered the nation of Israel.

Years later, Jesus came out of Galilee. Everyone in Israel looked down on the Galileans. That is why the Jewish leaders of his day, who came from the right families, who had all the education, looked down on Jesus and said, "Can any good thing come out of Nazareth?"

They could not receive Him, because they considered Him born in the wrong neighborhood. They didn't think He had the right pedigree.

What they didn't know about Jesus was that the blood flowing through His veins was far superior to theirs.

Who did Jesus pick as His disciples? Fishermen. Smelly, uneducated, ignorant fishermen. To make it worse, Galilean fishermen. Jesus took these men—Peter, James, John, and the others, and by God's power, He translated them from the kingdom of darkness into the kingdom of His son. (Colossians 1:13) Jesus infused them with His knowledge and His wisdom. And with these men He changed the course of history.

We are no different; all of us were in the kingdom of darkness. Jesus came to us and changed us. He came to you where you were, but He didn't leave you there. He reached down to where you were and pulled you out of the kingdom of darkness, where your heritage was total defeat, and He brought you into a new kingdom, His kingdom.

Jesus is now infusing you with His knowledge, His wisdom, and His ability. He is ripping off the chains of bondage in your life. He is bringing you into the light.

Now, through Him in you, you can and will change the course of history. You will do it.

Don't let the devil sell you those lies anymore. Surely, it would have been great to have had all those things that you consider plusses. But greater is He that is in you than all of your shortcomings. From the beginning of His dealings with men, God has used people who knew nothing. Through them, He has changed the course of nations. He has chosen people who, from all outward appearances, were total failures.

God has given you a new nature, a new mind, a new law, a new heritage to live by, a new spirit, a new song to sing. We are not singing an old song of defeat. We are singing the new song of victory.

You can have what it takes to be a leader!

Read books about men and women who have been successful in life. You will discover that the vast majority of them, while they were running the race to obtain the prize, had to overcome obstacles. They had to go on, oftentimes in spite of great handicaps. They had to overcome what seemed to be insurmountable problems.

I agree that there are people in the world today who are very successful financially, and they have done absolutely nothing to get that success. They were born with silver spoons in their mouths.

Those people are here, but we must face some facts. First, most of us are not like that. Second, most of us do not have a rich relative who will leave us millions of dollars. In addition, having lots of money is not the key to abundant life.

You can live your life without compromise. You can have the abundant life that Jesus came to give you. You can have the life of God in your life. But it would not be fair if I didn't tell you that, sooner or later, you must overcome obstacles in your life. If you are under the impression that all of these good things are going to happen to you just by reading this book and going to church, you are wrong.

If you are going to run to obtain the prize, you will be put to the test. God will not test you, but you will be put to the test. You will have to prove this Word in your life. You will have to put it to the test in your life. Don't be afraid of that, because you can win. You not only can win, but you will win!

And you will be challenged. Satan will throw the glove of challenge in your face. He knows what you are doing in your life. He knows what God says about you. He knows what you can be, what you can have, and what you can achieve in your life. He knows it better than we do. He knows what we can do, for he has seen people ahead of us do it.

Sooner or later, the devil will challenge you. He will challenge what you believe. He will challenge the commitment which you say you have made. He will make you fight for the ground you are gaining in this race.

When I made a decision to accept Jesus as my Lord, I thought I could receive Him and no one would ever know. It was amazing how many people found out. I merely wanted to take one step. That was the only part of the race I wanted to run. I just wanted to go to heaven. I was satisfied with that.

But I'll tell you, it seemed, when I took that step, the whole world exploded around me. People who were my friends were no longer my friends. All kinds of problems seemed to compound because I made that decision.

When you take the first step to obtain the prize, the devil will challenge you. The devil will try to make you compromise your step. He wants you to say, "Maybe I really don't want to do this." The devil will throw obstacles in front of you. The devil wants you to back down, "for you are the light of the world, the salt of the earth. (Matthew 5:13-14)

I believe you are a bright light in the earth. I believe you are salty.

Chapter VIII

DRESSED FIT TO RUN

10 Finally, my brethren, be strong in the Lord, and in the power of his might.

11 Put on the whole armour of God.... (Ephesians 6:10-11)

You are running a race. So many leaders really have a hard time in this area of running the race to win the prize—fighting the good fight of faith. They seem to get bogged down in their minds.

The Bible says to run the race to win the prize. As a leader, it must be your goal to win the prize. You must be in the front, so you can be seen.

Many leaders think they cannot be meek, fight the good fight of faith, run to win the prize, and stand on the Word, all at the same time. But Leviticus says that Moses was the meekest man in the whole earth, and he was also a man of power, strength, and no compromise.

Meekness is a fruit of the spirit. (Galatians 5:22-23) The word "meekness" means to trust in God's power, instead of your own. The literal definition of the word "meekness" in the Greek is "to not exert yourself." You cannot be a self-promoter. You must be a Jesus-promoter.

Ephesians 6:10 tells us to be strong in two ways. Be strong in the Lord, and be strong in the power of His might.

God wants you to be strong. The people you lead want you to be strong.

To be strong in the Lord is to be strong in the Word, for the Lord and His Word cannot be separated.

How do you become strong in the Word?

You must spend time in the Word. If you will get into the Word, you will get strong.

You need to become strong in the Lord. There is no limit to His strength. There is no boundary limiting the extent of His strength. His strength in your life can cause you to overcome the circumstances around you.

You must make the decision to put your confidence in Him. Then His strength will be in you.

He also said to be strong in the power of His might. It is good to know that His power can be in your life.

For I am not ashamed of the gospel of Christ: for it is the power of God unto salvation to every one that believeth.... (Romans 1:16)

Everyone means **you** are the one. The power of God is the gospel, and the gospel is the Word. The Word is God's power. If you will believe what is written, it doesn't matter what is in your life. It doesn't matter what

Dressed Fit To Run

is wrong with your body. It doesn't matter what is wrong with your head. The Word has within it the power of God unto salvation. The Word will produce in your life everything that Jesus purchased for you through His death, burial, and resurrection.

His Word is the power of God unto the salvation that Jesus provided, if you will believe it. It will release its power into your life, if you will release it.

I don't care what the doctor said, God has not met anything that is incurable. There is power in this gospel to set you free, if you will believe.

Where is the power? It is in the gospel.

10 Finally, my brethren, be strong in the Lord, and in the power of his might.

11 Put on the whole armour of God.... (Ephesians 6:10-11)

You are running in a race. How are you going to run a race with armor on? Anyone can tell you that you do not run races wearing armor.

But you should run this race wearing armor, for this is not a friendly race. Enemies are trying to destroy you while you run.

The thief cometh not, but for to steal, and to kill, and to destroy.... (John 10:10)

God has given you his armor to wear while you are running. You wear armor to a fight or battle. It's one thing to go out and run a race, but it's something else to run the race with armor on.

Everyone in the world is running the same race we are running—the race of life. When you go to the track with armor on, those people without armor will laugh at you. They realize you are running the same race they are running. They show up to run the race unencumbered, and you have on armor. But remember; the same enemy who is out to destroy you is out to destroy them. When you come running by, and they are lying on the roadside wounded, you will understand why God said to wear armor.

It may look as if you are falling behind because you made the decision to do things according to God's Word. It may look as if your ungodly friends and business associates are getting ahead of you. In fact, for a while, they may get ahead of you in some areas of life, because they are not encumbered by the laws of God. But when the enemy shows up, you will be prepared, and they will be washed away.

God is not going to come down to fight your battles. You have the armor. God has already produced everything we need. We do not need to go to the throne room of God, beating on His throne and saying, "God, please give me this!"

He has already produced it. It is already here. Everything we need in our lives is already in the earth. All of the help, all of the peace, all of the joy, all of the strength, everything we will ever need has already been birthed by God in the spirit realm. All we need to do is to believe His promises, act upon His Word, and do what He says.

If you act upon God's Word and keep His commandments, those things He has already birthed for you will find their way to your house. They will come upon you and overtake you. (Deuteronomy 28:1-2)

Dressed Fit To Run

Paul said, *Put on the whole armour of God....*
Why?
...That you may be able to stand against the wiles of the devil.

Stand against his schemes, plans, and ideas. Notice, he did not say to leave off those pieces that you don't like. He said to put on the whole armor.

Many people don't want to put on certain parts of this armor. I'll never understand why people don't want everything God wants them to have. God gave you armor because you have an enemy, an adversary. *Put on the whole armour of God, that ye may be able to stand against the wiles of the devil.*

Satan will try to steal your faith from you. He wants to take away from you the ability to believe God. Your faith is the pearl of great price. It is the most valuable thing you possess. Nothing you have in your life is more valuable than the ability to believe God. Satan wants to steal, through circumstances, situations, tests, trials, or problems, your ability to believe God. He wants to make you think it is foolish to believe the promises.

If he can get you to believe it will not work, then he will beat you. Don't let him fool you anymore.

Submit yourselves therefore to God. Resist the devil, and he will flee from you. (James 4:7)

The word "flee" means "to run from in stark terror."

Here is something you need to know about standing against the wiles of the devil. **People are not your enemies.**

For we wrestle not against flesh and blood, but against principalities, against powers, against

> *the rulers of the darkness of this world, against spiritual wickedness in high places.* (Ephesians 6:12)

We are using spiritual weapons against spiritual forces to achieve spiritual results. Satan loves to bog Christians down in fighting other people. People do the things they do because of the spiritual wickedness in the earth.

Ephesians 6:13 repeats verse 11. Every time you come to a place in the Bible where God repeats Himself within two or three verses, stop and read it again. He is repeating it for emphasis.

> *Wherefore take unto you the whole armour of God, that ye may be able to withstand in the evil day, and having done all, to stand.* (Ephesians 6:13)

You are going to stand until you overcome. And how do you overcome?

> *Whosoever believeth that Jesus is the Christ is born of God....* (1st John 5:1)

You are a whosoever, who believes that Jesus is the Christ, so you are born of God.

> *For whatsoever is born of God overcometh the world; and this is the victory that overcometh the world, even our faith.* (1st John 5:4)

You are a world overcomer! You have the ability birthed into you by God to overcome the world. There is nothing, absolutely nothing that Satan can throw against you, which you cannot overcome by believing the gospel. I don't care what the circumstances look like, you can change them, if you believe the gospel.

How do you believe?

You make the decision to believe, then you act upon it. You make the decision that you are going to believe the Word. Then you start putting the Word into your heart. You start building your life upon it. When the devil comes against you, you stand against him.

And how do you stand against him?

Tell him to be quiet, and start quoting scripture to him. Tell him, "No, you are not going to do this to me!"

Satan wants to steal your faith, your ability to believe God. He does it through circumstances and situations. Sometime in your life, you will come to a point where what you read in the Bible and what you see in your life are different. You will have to fight for what you believe in. The Bible says in one translation "to stand your ground." You have been delivered from the authority of darkness. Colossians 1:13 says you have been translated into the kingdom of God's dear Son. In that kingdom you have rights, and you have ground to stand on. You are not defenseless. You can whip Satan. Put on the armor and attack!

Stand therefore, having your loins girt about with truth.... (Ephesians 6:14) In Paul's day, everywhere he looked, Roman soldiers were standing on corners. Paul describes the Roman armor in the light of God's armor. In those days, men wore what we today would call a long skirt. It came down slightly below their knees. When they went into battle, they would reach down, grab the skirt, pull it up between their legs, wrap it around their waist, and tuck it in tightly. It gave them support around the waist.

Jesus said, ...*ye shall know the truth, and the truth shall make you free.* He told us to be girded (undersupported) with truth.

...And having on the breastplate of righteousness. That is one of the most important parts of the armor. Yet, many leaders will not put it on. Some say, "But Charles, the Bible says there is none righteous, and all have fallen short of the glory of God, and our righteousness is as filthy rags."

Yes, the Bible does say that about sinners, but it says this of us.

For he hath made him to be sin for us, who knew no sin; that we might be made the righteousness of God in Him. (2nd Corinthians 5:21)

You were unrighteous. You had fallen short of the glory of God. Your righteousness was as filthy rags. But God didn't leave you that way.

Through the new birth and your union with Christ, you have been made the righteousness of God. You will never be the leader God needs, if you reject your right-standing with Him. Righteousness is the ability to stand in the presence of God.

He compared righteousness to a breastplate. Back in Paul's day, they made the breastplates beautiful. They were intricately carved so that the men wearing them looked like supermen. That is what the devil sees when he looks at you, established in your right standing with God. He sees that breastplate of righteousness.

And your feet shod with the preparation of the gospel of peace. (Ephesians 6:15) That means, everywhere

Dressed Fit To Run

you go, you are supposed to be spreading peace—not strife, not fighting, not arguing, not contention, not division.

Above all, taking the shield of faith, wherewith ye shall be able to quench all the fiery darts of the wicked. (Ephesians 6:16) People ask me why I teach on faith so often. Here is the answer: so they will be able to quench all the fiery darts of the wicked.

All of the great leaders in the Bible and throughout history were men and women of faith. They believed in God, and they believed in themselves. No one will follow someone who doesn't believe in what they are attempting to do.

And take the helmet of salvation.... How do you take the helmet of salvation? You become more convinced of salvation than anything else, by meditating in the Word.

...And the sword of the Spirit, which is the word of God. (Ephesians 6:17)

For the word of God is quick, and powerful, and sharper than any twoedged sword.... (Hebrews 4:12)

The great thing about this sword is that it is alive. You can be fighting from behind your shield, and when you get tired, let the sword fight for a while. It is a living thing, full of power—and you can use it.

Meditate on the pieces of this armor. Develop your understanding of them. As you meditate on scriptures that speak about this armor, the reality of each piece will grow in your life. In order to lead people into battle, you must be dressed for battle. Thank God, you have the finest battle equipment available—the whole armor of God!

Chapter IX

THE DECISION IS YOURS

God has placed authority, dominion, and the right and the power to choose your own destiny into your hands. You can go to heaven if you want, and you can go to hell if you want.

You can be a leader or a follower, a winner or a loser. The choice is yours. God will not make it for you. God has already decided and declared what you can and should be. He has placed before you life and death, blessing and cursing; therefore choose life.

Christianity is a series of decisions. Every day, all day, you are making decisions about your life.

All leaders must be able to make decisions. Today you will make decisions about your life. Those decisions will determine the level of God's blessing and involvement in your life.

God has given you His Word to help you make those decisions, but He will not make them for you. He cannot make them for you. Neither can anyone else. They are yours to make, and yours alone. And the more responsibility you have, the more decisions you have to make.

You make different kinds of decisions on different levels. There are different qualities of decisions.

Many people make one decision because they are talking to you. If another person came along, they would make a different decision.

That is what is known as a double-minded man. James said that a double-minded man is unstable in all his ways and cannot receive anything of the Lord. (James 1:7-8)

15 I know thy works, that thou art neither cold nor hot: I would thou wert cold or hot.

16 So then because thou art lukewarm, and neither cold not hot, I will spue thee out of my mouth. (Revelation 3:15-16)

Either be yes or no, right or wrong, but don't be in the middle. I believe indecisiveness is the curse of America today.

Being a leader revolves around making decisions. If you aren't making decisions, then you are doing nothing. You cannot stay in the middle. Too many people try to walk the fence.

Leaders must get off the fence. People should know what their leaders stand for, what they believe in.

I have watched pastors try to keep everyone happy in their congregations.

Do you know what happens?

Everyone ends up angry with the pastor.

Why?

He was not setting the standard for the people to live by. Their leader was uncommitted and wavering, and that caused them to be anxious and fretful. Satan will try to keep you from making decisions. You are made in the image and the likeness of God. Since Satan cannot get to God, he will try to get to you.

We are caught in the middle. But God has not left us here defenseless. He has not put us on this planet at Satan's mercy. He has given us weapons which we can fight with.

The devil does not want you to obtain life. He does not want you to have God's power in your life. When you start walking in the fulness of God's power, you will start controlling him. He does not want you to control him.

If you control him in your life, you can control him in someone else's life. He is an outlaw, and he wants to run free through the earth. He wants to do what he wants to do, when he wants to do it, and how he wants to do it.

If you stand up to Satan, he will threaten you. He will try to bully you and frighten you. But you do not have to be afraid of him, because ...*greater is he that is in you, than he that is in the world.* (1st John 4:4)

God has given you the power to determine your destiny. If you are going to be a leader, you must make the decision that your confidence is in God's strength, and in His might, not in the arm of the flesh.

You have to put your confidence in God. That requires a decision. We are to be strong in the Lord, and in the power of His might.

To become strong in the Lord, you must become strong in the Word. The only way to become strong in The

Leadership: You Can Have What It Takes

Word is to go to church, listen to tapes, read good books, spend time in prayer, confess the Word of God, read the Word, meditate. Make the decision that you are going to become strong in God.

You need to do these things if you want to be a leader. There are no short-cuts. If you do not want to be the best leader you can be, then make decisions of lesser quality, but you will not be the kind of leader I am talking about.

If that is your decision, fine. But don't come to me saying that God is holding your life down and restricting your influence, because He is not.

The quality of your decision determines the quality of your life. You do not have to be sick or broke. You do not have to live in fear. You do not have to have mental problems, emotional problems, or social problems.

Since the Bible means what it says, you do not have to have those things in your life. Jesus will take care of you. He will meet your needs.

One of the greatest things you will learn in becoming a leader is to quit feeling sorry for yourself. To be a leader, you must give up having "pity parties."

If you think you have it so hard and get so tired, and no one has it as bad as you do, you are wrong. Quit feeling sorry for yourself. You are in a fight, and the devil is swinging at you.

If you stand there long enough, he will literally beat you to death. Or, you can get fed up and attack him!

Satan wants to take away your authority and leadership. He wants to steal your leadership from you. One way he will try is by telling you that the Word is not working for you. I tell you it **is working**. As long as heaven and earth are here, the Word is working.

Jesus said it was easier for heaven and earth to pass away then for one part of the Word not to come to pass. If you can open your window and see the earth, then God's Word is still working.

Satan will try to steal your faith in God and in yourself. He wants to take away your confidence in God's Word. He wants to steal from you so that you will lie down and let him walk right over you. He likes to steam-roller people. Make the decision that he cannot do those things to you.

27 Only let your conversation be as it becometh the gospel of Christ: that whether I come and see you, or else be absent, I may hear of your affairs, that ye stand fast in one spirit, with one mind striving together for the faith of the gospel:

28 And in nothing terrified by your adversaries: which is to them an evident token of perdition, but to you of salvation, and that of God. (Philippians 1:27-28)

The word "becometh" means "suitable and necessary." He said our conversation is to be that which is suitable to the gospel of Christ and necessary to the gospel of Christ.

One Greek text says "in nothing teffified" means "not caring two straws." The word "adversary" means "an enemy who fights determinedly, continuously, and relentlessly." It is also defined as being " a legal opponent."

Leadership: You Can Have What It Takes

The devil is determined, consistent, and relentless. But there is a place in

Christ where the devil fears to tread. The word "terrified" is the key word about adversaries—about your enemies.

Don't be afraid of what the devil is trying to do to you. Stand up on the inside. Let God's Word rise up within you. Turn on the devil and tell him to get out of your life!

Make your decision today how you are going to live. Then make it happen through faith in God's Word, absolutely refusing to back down!

Chapter X

FAITHFULNESS AND INTEGRITY

We are going to discuss some truths from the Bible that we **must** have in our lives, if we are to see the fullness of God's blessings upon us as leaders.

To be leaders, God's blessings must be in our lives. Remember, the people told Joshua they would follow him, if God was with him.

I have found that two of the most important criteria for God's blessings to be upon us are faithfulness and integrity. Without them you will never amount to very much. God cannot do much with people who are unfaithful or who lack intergrity.

When I say "faithfulness," most people think of a husband-wife relationship. Are they faithful to their spouse?

Faithfulness in our time carries a very limited definition, compared to what it meant when the King James translation was written. The word "faithful' means "to be strict or thorough in a task that you set out to accomplish or to do.' It also means "to be trusted and reliable." People can trust you. You are reliable. People can depend upon you to accomplish something when you set out to do it. In Proverbs 28:20 the Bible says, "A faithful man shall abound with blessing...."'

We are talking about these things because I want to see God's blessings in your life individually, and in our lives collectively as the church. You cannot survive in leadership without God's blessings. You cannot make it without the blessing of God—I promise you that.

Our church in El Paso is so dependent upon the Holy Ghost blessing for what we do that if He removed Himself from the inner workings of our church, it would collapse immediately. He holds our church together. He is in authority. We do not do things just because we think they are good ideas. We check them out with Him first. If He does not say "do it," we don't do it. I don't care how good it looks. Until we get the witness in our spirit that it is all right with the Holy Ghost, we do not do it. For that reason, at times, we tend to move very slowly, thus causing people to think we are hesitating.

No, we are not hesitating. We are allowing the light of the Holy Ghost to shine upon our feet before we start walking.

You can do many things which look good on paper, but you had better make sure the Holy Ghost tells you to do them. Check it out with Him. He knows things you do

Faithfulness And Integrity

not know. He understands things that you do not understand. He has insight that you do not have. And He wants to share that insight with you. He wants to give it to you.

Jesus said, ...*the Spirit of truth is come, he will guide you into all truth....* (John 16:13) Not some of the truth, not most of the truth, but all of the truth.

Jesus wants you to know things—do you realize that? He does not want you to walk around in darkness all the days of your life. He wants you to be wise. He wants you to walk in the wisdom and the counsel and the understanding of God. He wants you to have insight into things, and understand what life is about. Jesus said, *I am come that they might have life, and that they might have it more abundantly.* (John 10:10)

Faithfulness is vitally important to us as individuals, and as the Body of Christ, and as leaders.

In Matthew 25:14-30 Jesus gives us a teaching on faithfulness. This is the parable of the talents.

14 For the kingdom of heaven is as a man travelling into a far country, who called his own servants, and delivered unto them his goods.

15 And unto one he gave five talents, to another two, and to another one; to every man according to his several ability; and straightway took his journey.

16 Then he that had received the five talents went and traded with the same, and made them other five talents.

17 And likewise he that had received two, he also gained other two.

18 But he that had received one went and digged in the earth, and hid his lord's money.

19 After a long time the lord of those servants cometh, and reckoneth with them.

20 And so he that had received five talents came and brought other five talents, saying, Lord, thou deliveredst unto me five talents: behold, I have gained beside them five talents more.

21 His lord said unto him, Well done, thou good and faithful servant: thou hast been faithf over a few things, I will make thee ruler over many things: enter thou into the joy of thy lord.

22 He also that had received two talents came and said, Lord, thou deliveredst unto me two talents: behold, I have gained tow other talents beside them.

23 His lord said unto him, Well done, good and faithful servant; thou hast been faithful over a few things, I will make thee ruler over many things: enter thou into the joy of thy lord.

24 Then he which had received the one talent came and said, Lord, I knew thee that thou art an hard man, reaping where thou hast not sown, and gathering where thou hast not strawed:

25 And I was afraid, and went and hid thy talent in the earth: lo, there thou hast that is thine.

26 His lord answered and said unto him, Thou wicked and slothful servant, thou knewest that

I reap where I sowed not, and gather where I have not strawed:

27 Thou oughtest therefore to have put my money to the exchangers, and then at my coming I should have received mine own with usery.

28 Take therefore the talent from him, and give it unto him which hath ten talents.

29 For unto every one that hath shall be given, and he shall have abundance: but from him that hath not shall be taken away even that which he hath.

30 And cast ye the unprofitable servant into outer darkness: there shall be weeping and gnashing of teeth. (Matthew 25:14-30)

Notice that Jesus said, *For as the kingdom of heaven is....* The kingdom of heaven operates on the truths revealed in this parable. Jesus has delivered unto each of us talents according to our own particular abilities. Each member of the body of Christ has responsibilities. We each have areas that we need to look after and take care of, just as did the servants spoken of in the parable. Note that two of the servants took their talents or abilities and increased their effectiveness. They had faith that they could be productive with what they had been given. But one of the servants allowed fear to stop him from doing anything.

Today, we can see the same thing all around us. People are doing great things with the abilities and opportunities which the Lord has given them.

Leadership: You Can Have What It Takes

On the other hand, there are those hiding in the corner, afraid to take a stand.

I want you to remember how Jesus reacted to these servants, because His reactions are the same today.

Jesus Christ the same yesterday, and today, and forever. (Hebrews 13:8)

The servants who used their talents to increase were called good and faithful servants because they had been faithful over a little, and He made them rulers over much. The servant who did nothing was called a wicked, slothful servant, and he lost everything. If given a choice, I believe all of us would rather be counted among the good and faithful servants.

You may be asking, "How does this apply to leadership?"

I am constantly told by men and women that God has called them to do great things in the kingdom of God. But few of them ever make it.

Why?

Everywhere I go to teach, at least one person tells me they are called to preach, and then asks me what they should do to get into the ministry.

My answer sometimes surprises them. I tell them to start where they are, and be faithful over anything God gives them to do.

Before you can do great things, you must learn how to do small things.

Before you will stand before multitudes and declare the gospel, you will stand before a few and declare the gospel. Please, do not misunderstand what I am saying. I believe in having great visions and doing great things for God. But you must be faithful over little before you can rule much. If you do not learn how to be faithful over little, then much will rule you. And that is contrary to God's way of doing things.

When I answered the call to ministry, I told the Lord I would preach anywhere He opened a door, and to anyone. That same week, my pastor called me and asked me if I would take the three-and four-year-old class on Sunday nights.

I couldn't believe it! That was definitely not what I had in mind. I saw myself on a platform, behind the pulpit, with thousands of people sitting before me, hanging on my every word. No, three-and four-year-olds were definitely not what I had in mind.

I started to tell the pastor, "No", when the Lord said in my heart, "Anywhere? Anyone? Are not those little ones anyone?"

I was caught, and I knew it. I quickly told my pastor, "Yes," and began teaching that week.

God blessed me in that class, and I learned a great lesson about myself and others. I made myself faithful over little, and now I am a ruler over much.

Many people who desire to be leaders are envisioning spotlights and authority. Authority comes with responsibility. Do not seek after authority in your church or job. Accept responsibility, and authority will follow.

Look now at Luke 16:12.

And if ye have not been faithful in that which is another man's, who shall give you that which is your own? (Luke 16:12)

Solomon said that promotion does not come from the north, south, east or west, but it comes from God. If you ever expect God's promotion to come into your life, then you must learn this truth. If you want God to bless any area of your life, then you will need to be faithful over what He has already given you. He is not going to give you any more, if you are not taking care of what you already have, and cannot handle what He has already given you.

Before we go any further, I want to point out something else. When you read a verse of scripture like this, the thought could come—which I want to nip now—that if you are not in business or ministry for yourself, then you are not really walking in the fullness of God's blessing.

God will give you your own responsibilities to take care of. They will be your own responsibilities, even though you are not in business or ministry for yourself. I want you to see that you need to be faithful over that which God gives you.

Don't always be looking around thinking, "I'm going to be faithful right here, because God's going to give me my own business or ministry." That may not be God's will for your life. God's will for your life might be that you stay right where you are. He will bless you right there.

When you are in a situation where people begin to commit responsibility that was previously theirs into your hands, then God is beginning to promote you. You are being put into a position of authority. They are committing something that is theirs into your trust and keeping.

If you are faithful, God will move upon them to give you more. If they will not respond, God will move you somewhere else, if need be, to fulfill His Word. He may even move your boss.

Let's not try to figure it out. Just be obedient to His Word, taking care of things you set your hands to do.

...Jesus said unto him, No man, having put his hand to the plough, and looking back, is fit for the kingdom of God. (Luke 9:62)

He is saying, if you are going to do something, then do it! Paul said it like this in Colossians.

And whatsoever ye do, do it heartily, as to the Lord, and not unto men. (Colossians 3:23)

You may say, "Charles, what does this have to do with the deep things of Christianity?"

It has everything to do with it. The deep thing of Christianity is for you to let your light shine so that men will come out of the darkness into the light. If you want to see people come to your door and start knocking, be faithful over that which men commit into your trust.

The world is looking for that kind of person. I talk to business people all the time who are looking for someone who wants to do more than collect a paycheck.

Listen to me, church; this is the greatest hour the body of Christ has ever had. This is the greatest hour you have ever had to be a leader on your job, in your church, and in your community. Take the commands of God and walk in them, and do what He said. The Word says that a man's gift shall make a way for him.

A man's gift maketh room for him, and bringeth him before great men. (Proverbs 18:16)

But he that doeth truth cometh to the light, that his deeds may be made manifest, that they are wrought in God. (John 3:21)

I used to confess that scripture while I was teaching in small meetings—meetings of thirty or forty people. I remember times when Rochelle and I would drive twelve, thirteen, or fourteen hours to preach. Fifteen or twenty people would come. We would do five or six services in a weekend, but really, only one of those services would be worth our time.

When we went back to our hotel room, exhausted, the devil would be waiting for us. He never bothered us at the meeting. He would wait for us at the motel. As we came dragging in tired, and sat down to rest, he would be standing there saying, "What a waste of time!"

I wanted to say, "You're right."

We should then read the Word where it says they that are doers of the truth shall come to the light. Do you know what happens when we come to the light? It is manifested that your deeds are wrought in God, and you are soon promoted. You must be faithful over what God gives you.

INTEGRITY

Look now at integrity in a leader. If God can count on you to be faithful—if He knows, when He rings your number, you will answer and do what He asks of you—then you will see God promote you.

I am not talking about works. I am talking about being doers of the Word of God, being about our Father's business, so He can depend on us, so He can say, "I have this job to do over here and I'll just call Charles. He'll do it. He always does it."

God is looking for people who, when He speaks to their heart, will get up and do it. He is looking for people whom He can use.

I am not just talking about raising the dead and things like that. Those things are fine. But I am talking about people He can depend on daily.

In John the fourth chapter, Jesus said the Father seeks such to worship Him in spirit and in truth. When we think of worship, we generally think of a service where we sing and praise God. But there is a word, worship, in the Greek text for worship, seldom used, which is found only in the New Testament. It means this: "God is looking for people who will honor Him by doing menial tasks."

All kinds of people want to get into the spotlight. God needs people who will work behind the scenes and say, "I will do things. I will drive the car. I will hold the coat. I will vacuum the floor. I will do a good job right where I work every day. I will be a testimony to everyone that I can be trusted. I am a born-again child of the living God, and people can depend on me because of that. I am not flaky, I am not weird, but rather I am steady and consistent. I am dependable. On the job, when a dependable person is needed, they do not have to look any further than where I am standing."

God will use someone like that! God will do something for and through that person.

God has many people who have evangelistic associations, and they are running all over the country. There is no shortage of preachers. But God really needs workers

Leadership: You Can Have What It Takes

He can depend on at the gas company, and the electric company, and all other jobs.

That is where He needs Christians He can depend upon—people who are faithful. You have people around you that I will never contact. You are already in contact with them. It may take me two or three years to get to them. The moment they look at me and hear what I have to say, many will respond by saying, "Oh, it's just another preacher." They automatically do not believe half of what I say, and doubt half of the rest.

God is looking for people He can depend upon—people He can trust.

And as for me, thou upholdest me in mine integrity, and settest me before thy face for ever. (Psalms 41:12)

The dictionary defines "integrity" as "to have moral and ethical principles, soundness of moral character, honest."

We are studying faithfulness and integrity as they apply to leadership. Why are these things in the Bible? Why does God want us to be like this?

Notice what the Psalmist said. "The Lord upholds me because I adhere to moral and ethical principles." (Psalms 41:12) Adhere to them. That means to stick to them. We find the the reason why in Romans eight.

For whom he did foreknow, he also did predestinate to be conformed to the image of his Son, that he might be the firstborn among many brethren. (Romans 8:29)

For whom he did foreknow, he also did predestinate.... God has predestinated you to be something.

Faithfulness And Integrity

What is it? ...*to be conformed to the image of his Son, that he might be the firstborn among many brethren.* Verse 31 says, ...*If God be for us, who can be against us?* He has predestinated us to be conformed to the image of His dear Son. God wants you and me to be conformed to the image of His dear Son. He wants us to act like Jesus. Paul said in Ephesians 5:1, *Be ye therefore followers* (imitators) *of God...*

You and I cannot live a life contrary to God's character and God's way of doing things, and expect Him to bless and exalt you. You cannot purposely and knowledgeably live contrary to God's Word and then step over quickly to say, "Lord, You promised in Your Word that You would bless me." He will not do it.

God loves you. You will still go to heaven. But don't expect the blessings of God to flow in your life abundantly. You will see them to a certain extent, because the Bible does say the Lord causes the rain to fall on the just and the unjust. A certain amount of God's blessing will come into your life just because you are Christian. But you will not receive the supernatural flow. With this flow, the windows of heaven are opened up and blessings are poured out that there is not room enough to contain them.

> ...*prove me now herewith, saith the Lord of hosts, if I will not open you the windows of heaven, and pour you out a blessing, that there shall not be room enough to receive it.* (Malachi 3:10)

Are you ready to experience the flood tide of God's blessings?

Leadership: You Can Have What It Takes

I want to be where God is moving. I'm tired of hearing about what other people are doing. I want to do something myself for the kingdom of God. I want to see people's lives changed.

God is not a man, that he should lie... (Numbers 23:19)

God cannot lie. Everyone knows that. The man on the street who has never heard a verse of scripture in his life has heard somewhere that God cannot lie. What then would you say about God? God has integrity. He cannot lie.

I am going to build something here, and I want you to see it. Your entire life with Him is based on His integrity. Your entire relationship with God is based on His integrity. You believe what He said is the truth. If you didn't believe what He said is the truth, you wouldn't be reading this book, and there would be no way you could depend on Him. God is a being of integrity.

In John 8:44, Jesus said that Satan is the father of lies. So what we have here is a contrast. We have God, who is all truth. He is a God of integrity. You can depend upon what He says; it is the truth. Jesus said in John 8:32, *And ye shall know the truth, and the truth shall make you free.* Then He says in verse 44 that Satan is the father of lies and there is no truth in him. He said that so you and I would see the separation that exists between God and Satan. God is light. Satan is darkness. God is truth. Satan is lies.

Our entire relationship with God is based upon the fact that He is a God of integrity. In Jeremiah 1:12 God said, *...for I hasten my word to perform it.* That is integrity. If God says it, you can depend upon it.

Faithfulness And Integrity

God adheres to moral and ethical principles. He is honest. Psalms 119:89 says, *For ever, O Lord, thy word is settled in heaven.* Paul said it like this in Hebrews 13:8, *Jesus Christ the same yesterday, and today, and forever.* He is the same. He does not change His mind. He does not change His way of doing things. He does not change His way of acting. He does not change His way of talking or believing. He is the same. Because He is the same, because He is a God of integrity, you can depend upon Him. You can put your trust in Him. You will follow His lead. Solomon said you can trust in the Lord with all your heart. If God said it, you can depend upon it.

What about our integrity? The Bible says that we are to be conformed to the image of Jesus. We are to be imitators of God. God is a God of integrity. Ephesians 5:1 tells us to imitate Him. In other words, integrity is to be found in us. God wants you to act like Him.

He wants to build His character into your heart. God wants to take His character, His ways of doing things, the way He lives, the way He responds, and build these into your spirit. Then you can live like He lives, have what He has, and experience life on a higher plane than the rest of humanity, because you have purposed to be like Him.

Jesus said, "If you will give up the low life, I will give you the high life." The high life is living as He does, and acting as He acts. This takes time to learn. You plot a course to achievement in your life. If you become a person of integrity, things will happen for you.

The Lord shall judge the people: judge me, O Lord, according to my righteousness, and according to mine integrity that is in me. (Psalms 7:8)

The Lord shall judge the people.... We all know that God is going to judge humanity. That is His responsibility. He has taken that upon Himself. The Lord shall judge the people. *...Judge me, O Lord, according to my righteousness, and according to mine integrity that is in me.* That is a bold statement. But God wants us to be able to say the same thing. He wants the same reality in us.

The integrity of the upright shall guide them.... (Proverbs 11:3) "Charles, I don't know what to do. I'm in this situation, and I just do not know what to do. On the one hand, I ought to do this, but on the other hand, maybe I ought to do that. If I do this, it isn't illegal, but...."

What would integrity do?

If there is anywhere in the world where people should be able to find honesty, it should be in the body of Christ. God will not bless fraud. God will not bless lies. God will not bless dishonesty. He just will not do it. There is no room for those things in a leader's life.

You can walk around and confess the Word all day long. You can wear out your brand new carpet confessing that God is going to bless you, but as long as you are living without integrity, you can wear that carpet out, wear your shoes out, walk your legs off up to your knees, but He will not bless you.

Mark it down, write it down, and believe it. God will not bless you if you are dishonest. The standard of honesty is the Bible.

If you are not sure what direction to go, look at yourself and ask, "What would integrity do?" Do not lower yourself to the level of a spiritual con-artist.

I have seen people trick and con other people into giving them things. If you are believing God for something, He will get it to you before you have to pull a spiritual trick. I am not judging you, or picking on you. I am just trying to keep you out of trouble because I love you. I am trying to tell you how to get into the blessings of God.

Better is the poor that walketh in his uprightness, than he that is perverse in his ways, though he be rich. (Proverbs 28:6)

God says that a poor man with integrity has greater richness than a man who is wealthy, but lacks integrity. In the eyes of God, a poor man with integrity has something of greater value than an enormously wealthy man who is dishonest.

Someone once told me, "When I went into business, everyone told me that I had to play the game. I had to wine and dine people and get girls for them. I said, 'no', and they told me I would never get ahead. I told them that I would not do that. I do not believe in it."

He did not judge them. He did not get up on a spiritual high horse and look down his nose at them. He merely said, "I'm not going to do that."

This man is in an industry today where many people are going bankrupt, but he is still working. He said that people call him up to say, "You are more expensive than everyone else, but when you tell us you are going to to something, you do it."

God knows what He is talking about. Integrity is of great value in the eyes of God.

The just man walketh in his integrity: his children are blessed after him. (Proverbs 20:7)

Where does he walk?

In his integrity. Now look what happens. His children are blessed after him. If you don't care about yourself, do it for your children. If you don't care whether God ever uses you or not, do it for your children. If you can't do it for anyone else, then give them an example, a heritage that they can look up to and have something to live for. You are the greatest teacher your children have.

In First Kings 9, Solomon has built the temple and the Lord is talking to him.

> *4 And if thou wilt walk before me, as David thy father walked, in integrity of heart, and in uprightness, to do according to all that I have commanded thee, and wilt keep my statutes and my judgments:*
>
> *5 Then I will establish the throne of thy kingdom upon Israel for ever....* (1 Kings 9:4-5)

He will establish you also. David said that the Lord upholds him in his integrity. God is looking for people that He can put the light on and say, "Hey, world, look at this person."

Let's look at Job. He had two problems. His first problem was fear.

> *For the thing which I greatly feared is come upon me....* (Job 3:25)

His second problem was self-righteousness. As you read through the book of Job, you find Job becoming more and more self-righteous. Finally the Lord speaks to him out of a whirlwind and says, "Where were you when I made the heavens?"

Faithfulness And Integrity

A lot of people think that God did those bad things to Job. God did not do anything to Job. The devil did it.

Notice that while Job was minding his own business, in the course of about two weeks, the whole world caved in on him. He lost his sons and daughters, his cattle were killed, his house collapsed, and he came down with an incurable disease. Job had a problem.

Then said his wife unto him, Dost thou still retain thine integrity? curse God, and die. (Job 2:9)

That's a dumb solution, isn't it? Curse God. When you do that, you will really have problems.

But he said unto her, Thou speakest as one of the foolish women speaketh.... (Job 2:10)

The point I want you to see is that, even when something was happening to Job that he did not understand, he would not let go of his integrity. In a situation like that, most men would say, "This doesn't work. Serving God is not worthwhile." They would throw it down and do something else.

Even in Job's situation, he would not let go of his integrity. Most people would have quit.

Integrity is seen in two areas in your life—first in your words, and second in your deeds.

People see the integrity of your heart in your speech and in your actions. I cannot look into your spirit and see whether or not you have integrity. But I will know by your words and your deeds. That is what counts.

Set a watch, O Lord, before my mouth; keep the door of my lips. (Psalms 141:3)

Death and life are in the power of the tongue.... (Proverbs 18:21)

The psalmist asked the Lord to put a watch before his mouth. The psalmist David understood something here, didn't he?

A false witness shall not be unpunished, and he that speaketh lies shall perish. (Proverbs 19:9)

God does not bless lying.

Keep thy foot when thou goest to the house of God, and be more ready to hear, than to give the sacrifice of fools....

What is the sacrifice of fools?

...for they consider not that they do evil.

2 Be not rash with thy mouth....

James said that the wise man is slow to speak.

...and let not thine heart be hasty to utter any thing before God....

In other words, before you talk to Him about something, think about what you are going to say.

...for God is in heaven, and thou upon earth: therefore let thy words be few.

3 For a dream cometh through the multitude of business; and a fool's voice is known by multitude of words.

4 When thou vowest a vow unto God, defer not to pay it; for he hath no pleasure in fools: pay that which thou hast vowed. (Ecclesiastes 5:1-4)

Faithfulness And Integrity

I wonder how many people who are in trouble or in a tight spot say, "God, if you will just get me out of this I will never get drunk again... I will quit cussing... I will start going to church," and do not keep their word?

5 Better is it that thou shouldest not vow, than that thou shouldest vow and not pay.

6 Suffer not thy mouth to cause thy flesh to sin... (Ecclesiastes 5:5-6)

In other words, do not bite off more than you can chew. This is especially important as a leader. He is telling us to not say anything that we cannot keep our word on.

If you say you are going to do something, do it. Do not make decisions based upon emotions. Back up your words with your actions. Become dependable in every area of your life, so that people can depend upon your words.

In your home, on your job, with your friends, with your children, with your business associates, be dependable. If you say you are going to do something—do it! Learn to not make promises beyond your ability to perform.

Chapter XI

WOMEN, LEADERS, AND THE BIBLE

In this chapter we will address several of what I consider to be the most controversial scriptures in the Bible. Each scripture deals specifically with women, and their place in the church.

For years, there have been many heated debates over the role of women in the body of Christ, and their role in the ministry.

At times, the body of Christ has been guilty of talking out of both sides of its mouth. For example, we extol the leadership qualities of Esther. We teach our children about her courage and commitment, and tell them how she was used of the Lord to save her people. Then we say that a woman cannot teach, or pastor, or be in leadership positions.

Some have even gone so far as to say that it is wrong for a woman to work outside of the home. I would agree that upon first reading of the scriptures we are going to study, these opinions could be assumed.

However, with careful study of the original text, and reading it in the light of our redemption, coupled together with sound common sense, we can see and know the truth. The truth will set us free.

Some of this chapter will deal with women who are married. I believe the single readers will benefit from this almost as much as those who are married. If you are not married at this time, you may be in the future, and you will become involved with married people as you grow in leadership.

Because of the references to marriage in the scriptures we will be studying, I will begin by making some general remarks about God's plan for marriage. This will help us understand the things we will to be discussing. I believe you will be as convinced as I am that women **can** be and **should** be leaders in the body of Christ and in the world today.

God's plan and purpose in marriage is a harmonious union, where two people live together as one. This can be difficult, if two people are brought together into marriage from **totally** different backgrounds.

Television paints marriage as an idealistic situation where the couple has nothing but huggy, kissy, good times. I would venture to say that when you got married (or if you are contemplating marriage now) you had a dream of what marriage is supposed to be.

There is nothing wrong with that. The conflict sometimes arises when you discover that your mate's dreams and your dreams do not match. Suddenly there is a problem.

If you will spend time talking about the good points in your husband or wife, instead of magnifying the bad points, you will have a happier marriage. Before I got my life on track with the Lord, I worked at a steak house. Men would come in on Saturday night by themselves. Someone would always ask, "Hey, buddy, where's your wife?" And they would say, "I left the ball and chain at home tonight."

I didn't know then what I know now about marriage, but that bothered me. I felt sorry for those men. They thought of their wives as a ball and chain, something they had to drag around, as if their wives were dead weight.

They had funny ideas about what marriage was, and what responsibility was. Many of them did not want responsibility. The just wanted to cruise.

We play games—serious games—with one another in marriage. One of the biggest games played is when people put on a veneer and are not real with one another. Jesus wants you to be real. He wants you to be you.

Don't try to be what you think your husband or wife wants you to be. Be yourself. If there are things within you that are not good, don't be that way.

We need to realize that men and women are different in other than just sexual ways. Ladies, there are a lot of things in your life, important to you, that are not important to your husband. But don't get your feelings hurt, and don't cry about it.

A couple came to me one time with serious marital trouble. The whole problem centered around the fact that the wife thought her husband didn't love her any more.

The man sat in my office looking at me as if to say, "I don't know why I'm here."

I asked her, "How do you know your husband doesn't love you any more?"

She said, "Because he doesn't tell me he loves me, when he goes to work."

They had been married nine or ten years, and every morning before he went to work, he would tell her that he loved her. He had quit doing that for about five or six weeks, and she was convinced that he no longer loved her.

This was a real problem in that woman's life. It should not have been a real problem, but it was. I asked him why he didn't tell his wife that he loved her anymore.

He said," I don't know. But I'll start doing it tomorrow."

This is an extreme illustration, but the point is well made. You can allow molehills to become mountains in your marriage. If you center upon them and magnify them, they will grow and grow. And soon you have a huge problem.

You must be careful in your marriage. Before you let yourself get upset, sit down, look at the situation, and ask yourself, "Is this really worth getting upset over and getting in strife over? It is really that important for me to put my foot down and bring this to a confrontation?"

There are some things you must confront, but there are some things that really do not matter. If your spouse doesn't put shoes in the closet just the way you want it done, is that worth a fight? By the same token, is it worth a fight if you keep on doing something, knowing your spouse doesn't like it?

Why don't you quit being so mean and try to get along—change a little bit. Enough problems will come against your marriage without you creating some.

Don't allow things that amount to nothing to become things that amount to everything. At the same time, I am not saying that the woman needs to do all the giving, nor am I saying that the man needs to do all the giving. I am saying that both need to do all of the giving.

Marriage is 100% - 100%. It is not 50% - 50%. You need to be willing to give of yourself. You need to be willing to change. You should desire to work together, not to cause your husband or wife to get into strife. You are not going to get your way all the time. Realize that the person you are married to is a human being deserving respect, particularly if he or she is born-again child of God.

In Ephesians five, the apostle Paul says men are supposed to love their wives with the God kind of love. Men are to nourish and cherish their wives. Do you cherish your wife? Do you look upon her as someone who is valuable? You are the only one who can answer that.

If you cherish something, you will not do anything to harm it. You will not do anything to hurt it.

The book of Proverbs says that the man who has found a wife has found a good thing and has obtained favor from the Lord. When I read that scripture one night, a man sitting across the room said, "God, don't do me any more favors." It just came out of his heart. His eyes were so big as I looked over at him. He couldn't believe he said that.

Men have a responsibility in the family to teach their children.

And, ye fathers, provoke not your children to wrath: but bring them up in the nurture and admonition of the Lord. (Ephesians 6:4)

Men are usually the chief means of supply that God uses to meet the needs of the family. That does not mean that the man is the bread winner. Men, the greatest favor you will do for your family is to explain to them that Jesus is the bread-winner of your family. Take the pressure off yourself.

This does not mean that you should stay home and do nothing.

One of the literal definitions of the word "Lord" in Romans ten is "bread supplier." *If any man confess Jesus as Lord,* means to confess Him as your bread-supplier.

What did Jesus tell his disciples to pray to the heavenly Father?

"Give us this day our daily bread." God wants to be your bread-supplier. Let Him. He can do a better job of it than you.

If you will let Jesus become the bread-supplier in your family, you will not get under pressure if your job should change, because the source remains the same. He remains the same. Let Him take that position. He wants it. He is better at it, and He is more equipped.

What about the woman?

What about women as leaders in the church and in the world? We shall study some scriptures that have caused a lot of controversy.

1 Be ye followers of me, even as I also am of Christ.

2 Now I praise you, brethren, that ye remember me in all things, and keep the ordinances, as I delivered them to you.

3 But I would have you know, that the head of every man is Christ; and the head of the woman is the man; and the head of Christ is God. (1st Corinthians 11:1-3)

Notice he is talking about three different types of heads—the head of man, the head of woman, and the head of Christ.

A better translation of the head of the man would be the head of the husband, and head of the woman could be head of the wife. He said the head of the husband is Christ, the head of the wife is the husband, and the head of Christ is God.

The word "head" does not mean ruler. It literally means "seat of life." In the Oriental world, (which includes the Middle East) a man's or a woman's or an animal's head is considered to be the seat of life. The head is where the life of the being is. He said that the seat of life of every man is Christ. That is understandable—we draw our life from Christ.

Let me show you what some of the literal translations say. Paul shows us several special relationships, two of which are very easy to understand.

One, Christ is the seat of life for mankind; and two, God is the source of life for Jesus. But then he said that the husband is the source of life for the wife.

What type of life is he speaking of there—spiritual life? Is the husband the source of spiritual life for the wife?

No.

If that were the case, no woman could get born again until she was married. Then she would have to clear it with her husband, and go through him to become a Christian. If that were true, many women would have gone to hell waiting for their husbands to straighten up. What about the woman who did not marry? What would happen to her? She could never become a Christian.

If we stop to think about it for a few minutes, and remember that Jesus came to bring us liberty, not bondage, these things are not hard to understand.

My wife does not need to go through me to achieve spiritual results. Jesus is her seat of spiritual life.

Then the headship that I have must be a physical headship.

What arrangement could I have with my wife where I would be life supplier for her? You know what it is. You have been thinking about it since you were sixteen years old.

The husband definitely has something to do with his wife in fulfilling the desire she has to bear children. He is a seat of life to her in that situation.

Every man praying or prophesying, having his head covered, dishonoureth his head. (1st Corinthians 11:4)

That word "man" in verse four is a Greek word that literally means "everyone, regardless of sex." It is a word which has a universal application to man, woman, boy, or girl. There is no sexual distinction in the word. So the verse says that everyone (man or woman) who prays or prophesies, having his head covered, dishonors his head.

To really grasp the full meaning to this text, you need to understand the social and religious customs in the lives of the people this letter was written to.

Jewish men, under the law, always wore small caps on their heads. These were a constant reminder of the condemnation of sin. Jewish women never wore anything on their heads. Married Greek women in Corinth wore veils. The unmarried ones did not. If a woman had her head shaved, it was because she had been caught as a prostitute.

> *Every man praying or prophesying, having his head covered, dishonoureth his head....* (1st Corinthians 11:4)

He said every "person," but I want to read it in the masculine tense. Understanding that Christ is the seat of life for the male, if a male prayed with that cap on his head, then he was still reminding himself that he was under the condemnation of sin. That is dishonor to Jesus, isn't it? He came to free us from the condemnation of sin.

But every woman that prayeth or prophesieth with her head uncovered dishonoureth her head.... (1st Corinthians 11:5)

That is the same basic statement that he made in verse four, only reversed. In verse four, Paul said that a person, male or female, who prays or prophesies with his/her head covered dishonours his/her head.

In verse five he seems to contradict himself, for he says that every wife who prays or prophesies with her head uncovered dishonors her head, just as if she was shaven.

> *For if the woman be not covered, let her also be shorn: but if it be a shame....* (1st Corinthians 11:6)

This is the key verse. The word "but" should be translated "now." He says ...*now if it be a shame...* The word "if" is a word that you associate with doubt, isn't it? Paul is talking about social customs, not Bible doctrines.

But if any man (the word "man" is male or female) *seem to be contentious,* (about having your head covered or uncovered) *we have no such custom, neither the churches of God.* (1st Corinthians 11:16)

He is saying that it is not a custom anywhere but in Corinth. They were the only ones squabbling over the issue. He said if it is a shame for a woman to be shorn or shaven, let her be covered. He is talking about a local custom that occurred in Corinth.

In Corinth it was a shame to the husband if his wife went out in public without a veil on. It shamed him.

To paraphrase Paul, he said, "Look men, it does not matter to God whether you pray with your head covered or not; he would really rather you didn't. But if it embarrasses the husband for his wife to come into the church, remove her veil, and begin to pray, then go ahead and be covered. Avoid the strife."

He is not laying down a big Bible doctrine that says women must wear veils.

I have seen women under such bondage that if they came to church having forgotten their veils, they would find a napkin or a kleenex and pin it to the top of their heads. Do you think that is what Paul had in mind when he said these things? Should a woman wear a kleenex on her head when she goes into a church? Do you think it really matters in the kingdom of God if a woman has something on top of her head when she prays? Is that what is going to get you through to God?

All we need to do to understand this is to think about this for about fifteen seconds. Paul is talking about a social custom.

In chapter ten he said for us not to do anything that would cause another person to stumble.

Wherefore let him that thinketh he standeth take heed lest he fall. (1st Corinthians 10:12)

Paul is saying, "Women, if it is hard on your Corinthian husbands for you to come into the church and remove your covering or veil when you worship, pray, and prophesy, then leave yourselves covered."

If it is going to be a point of contention, and causes strife, then just avoid it. That makes more sense to me than women wearing napkins on their heads.

6 For if the woman be not covered, let her also be shorn: but if it be a shame for a woman to be shorn or shaven, let her be covered.

7 For a man indeed ought not to cover his head, forasmuch as he is the image and glory of God.... (1st Corinthians 11:6-7)

Is the male of the species the only one made in the image and glory of God?

No.

So God created man in his own image, in the image of God created he him; male and female created he them. (Genesis 1:27)

God made man, male and female, in His own image.

For a man indeed ought not to cover his head, forasmuch as he is the image and glory of God: but the woman is the glory of the man. (1st Corinthians 11:7)

The word "glory" pertains to an outward, physical, visual, shining force. This glory is something you can see. It is an outward shining. In verse seven he shows us that *...the woman is the glory of the man.* Paul was not in favor of women being covered up when they prayed and prophesied. He pointed out that there wasn't such a custom anywhere else in the churches of God.

The purpose of revealing some things to the Corinthians was to get them out of that foolishness.

Even as men are the glory of God, the woman is the glory of the man. Isn't that beautiful? Paul wants the men to understand that their wives are their glory. Your wife is the "shining forth" of you. Therefore, don't cover her up. Let her beauty shine forth.

For the man is not of the woman; but the woman of the man. (1st Corinthians 11:8)

Woman was made from man. It tells us so in Genesis two. That is not a putdown. It's a statement of fact.

Verse ten says, *"For this cause..."* Or, "For this reason...."

What reason?

The fact that the woman is the glory of the man. Your wife is to be a shining forth of your own excellence. When people look at my wife, they form a mental impression or image of me. If she is always walking around in worn-out clothes because I won't let her wear anything nice, that is a reflection on me.

The Bible says she is my glory. That is what it says. Since the wife is the glory of the husband, I say, "Fix her up."

I have never understood men who begrudge their wives wanting to look nice and wear nice clothes. When people look at her, they are looking at you also. The woman is the glory of the man. Isn't that beautiful?

Wives should remember that they are the glory of their husband. They are reflecting him. Think about that the next time you go down to the grocery store looking like something that came out from underneath a rock.

Many women, after they get married, think they no longer have to protect their investment. They think they can let themselves go and not fix themselves up anymore. They mistakenly think that the ring on their finger is a guarantee of eternal love and sexual attraction.

10 For this cause ought the woman to have power on her head because of the angels. (1st Corinthians 11:10)

For this cause (because the woman is the glory of the man) *ought the woman to have power on her head because of the angels.* Where did the angels come from? Paul is talking about husbands and wives, and suddenly angels pop up.

What do angels have to do with this? *For this cause ought the woman to have power...* That word "power" literally means "liberty and authority." It does not mean covering. It does not mean kleenex. *For this cause ought the woman to have liberty and authority.* That word "on" literally means "over."

Paul is actually making a rebuttal to the custom of the Corinthian men that their wives must always be covered up in veils. You could not see anything but their eyes. If a woman was not dressed that way, it meant she was single.

A married woman who went out uncovered shamed her husband. It meant that she was on the run.

Paul is writing into the midst of all that religious and social tradition. He made a statement about it, and then he did some teaching so the light of God could be shed on the subject and they could receive the truth. He could have come on like gangbusters, but he would have offended ninety percent of the men in the church. It was not their fault they believed that way. It was their custom. They had been raised in it all their lives.

Paul says, because the woman is your glory, she reflects you. She reflects your excellence. The woman ought to have liberty and authority over her own head. If she wants to be covered, fine; if she doesn't, fine.

But whatever she does, she should be doing it in respect to the desire of her own husband.

Then he puts in the tag—because of the angels. The Bible teaches that the angels learn about the wisdom and the counsel and the worship of God from men. Yes, they worship God—but not like men do.

God is searching for people to worship Him in spirit and in truth.

But the hour cometh, and now is, when the true worshippers shall worship the Father in spirit and in truth: for the Father seeketh such to worship him. (John 4:23)

God has millions of angels worshipping Him, and they do an excellent job of it. Why then is God looking for people to worship Him? Obviously, He is not satisfied with that type of worship. He wants our type of worship.

The angels are present with us in our services to watch and to be a part of what men are doing. Paul is saying, take off the veils (they hinder their worship), and let your wives worship God in spirit and in truth, so the angels can see it and glory in it.

11 Nevertheless neither is the man without the woman, neither the woman without the man, in the Lord.

12 For as the woman is of the man, even so is the man also by the woman; but all things of God.

13 Judge in yourselves: (the Greek text reads, "Judge for yourselves") *is it comely* (or is it fitting) *that a woman pray unto God uncovered?* (1st Corinthians 11:11-13)

You decide. If you think it is right, then it is right. If you think it is wrong, then it is wrong. Do whatever you want to do. Paul is telling them, judge for yourselves. Make your own decision. He knows what type of decision they would make after he taught them as he did.

Doth not even nature itself teach you, that, if a man have long hair, it is a shame unto him? (1st Corinthians 11:14)

Does nature teach us that? I am not contradicting Paul, but does nature teach you that a man should not have long hair? If anything, nature teaches you that in many animals the males have longer hair than the females, e.g. lions.

What is he talking about then? Nature really has nothing to do with whether your hair is long or not—you do. A man's hair does not grow to a certain length and then stop growing.

15 But if a woman have long hair, it is a glory to her... (1st Corinthians 11:15)

The word "long" does not appear in the Greek text, and the word "hair" is a Greek word that is literally translated "ornamental hair." Again you have to read it somewhat in the light of the custom about which it was written.

Back in those days, the men of different social standards would spend many hours fixing their hair in a very ornamental way. It separated them from the lower classes.

One fashion of the day for the men was to gather all the hair up and wear it right on their forehead. They did it that way because they believed that was how the Greek god Apollos wore his hair.

He is saying it is not right for a man to wear this ornamental hair as a means of class separation.

Why?

Because in Christ there isn't any difference.

There is neither Jew nor Greek, there is neither bond nor free, there is neither male nor female: for ye are all one in Christ Jesus. (Galatians 3:28)

Paul said that if a woman had ornamental hair, it is a glory to her. If a woman takes time fixing her hair to make it look nice and to wear it in a pretty fashion, it is a glory to her. It makes more sense the more I read it.

SILENCE

27 If any man (the word "man" means "male or female") *speak in an unknown tongue, let it be by two, or at the most by three, and that by course; and let one interpret.*

28 But if there be no interpreter, let him keep silence in the church; and let him speak to himself, and to God.

29 Let the prophets speak two or three, and let the other judge.

30 If any thing be revealed to another that sitteth by, let the first hold his peace.

31 For ye may all prophesy one by one.... (1st Corinthians 14:27-31)

Does "all" mean all male and all female?

Yes, it does.

31 For ye may all prophesy one by one, that all may learn, and all may be comforted.

32 And the spirits of the prophets are subject to the prophets.

33 For God is not the author o confusion, but of peace, and in all churches of the saints. (1st Corinthians 14:31-33)

What is God the author of in the churches?

Peace.

34 Let your women keep silence in the churches: for it is not permitted unto them to speak; but they are commanded to be under obedience, as also saith the law. (1st Corinthians 14:34)

Do not read verse 34 our of context. Read it in the light of redemption. He said that everyone could prophesy. Would he say everyone could prophesy in verse 31, but then in verse 34 say the women have to be quiet? Obviously, he is not saying what we think he is saying.

Not one verse of scripture in the Levitical law says that women must keep quiet in church. Paul was speaking of the Rabbinical law given to the Jews by the Rabbi, written in addition to the law that God gave through Moses. It was not inspired by God.

In the Rabbinical law it was written that when a man awoke in the morning, and before he got out of bed, he was to say, "God, I thank you that I was not born a woman." That is how the Rabbi felt about women, and that idea is still in the world today.

Some of you may have been brought up in an atmosphere where your father, grandfather, and uncles all wished for a boy instead of a girl. They almost treated the girls as though they were a curse instead of a blessing.

It is just as real today as it was then. Paul is not talking about a commandment of God. He is talking about something the Corinthians were doing. It was not based upon the teachings and laws of God.

The understated subject of verse 34 is the word "you." This sentence is a statement of fact, not a command. If read like that, it says, "You let your women keep silence in the churches." He is not commanding them, he is rebuking them.

He just got through saying in the previous verses that all were to prophesy. Then he says, but you Corinthians make your women be silent in the church because you say the law commands them to be under obedience.

It was not the law of God that said that—it was the law of men!

35 And if they will learn any thing, let them ask their husbands at home: for it is a shame for women to speak in the church. (1st Corinthians 14:35)

The church has built some far-out doctrines with that verse. Thousands of Christian women have never been allowed to fulfill the calling of God in their lives because of erroneous thinking about that verse.

36 What? came the word of God out from you? or came it unto you only? (1st Corinthians 14:36)

Paul is rebuking them. He is asking them if they were the ones who came up with the Word of God. Were they the ones who received the revelations, or did it come unto them only?

37 If any man think himself to be a prophet, or spiritual, let him acknowledge that the things that I write unto you are the commandments of the Lord,

38 But if any man be ignorant, let him be ignorant.

39 Wherefore, brethren, (that word "brethren" is a Greek word that means "brothers and sisters") *covet to prophesy, and forbid not to speak with tongues.* (1st Corinthians 14:37-39)

Paul tells us that a woman, as well as a man, can prophesy and speak in tongues in the church.

Why would he change what he said in verses 34 and 35? Obviously he was not writing a commandment to them. He pointed out an error to them and rebuked them for their thinking in that area. He told them they were wrong. They got those ideas about women from the Rabbinical law.

Think about it from a practical level, and it will make sense to you.

BUT WOMEN CAN'T TEACH

8 I will therefore that men pray every where, lifting up holy hands, without wrath and doubting.

9 In like manner also, that women adorn themselves in modest apparel, with shamefacedness and sobriety; not with broided hair, or gold, or pearls, or costly array.

10 But (which becometh women professing godliness) with good works.

11 Let the woman learn in silence with all subjection.

12 But I suffer not a woman to teach, nor to usurp authority over the man, but to be in silence. (1st Timothy 2:8-12)

I am going to give you some more literal definitions. This is what the Word says. He said, *In like manner also, that women adorn themselves in modest apparel with shamefacedness....* That word "modest" means "orderly or sober."

Somehow men believe that verse means "without makeup." Wearing makekup or not wearing makeup makes no difference to God. If that is what you want to do, do it.

The word "shamfacedness" does not mean "without makeup." It means "reverence and sobriety."

The word "sobriety" means "discretion." He is telling Christian women to dress orderly. The word "apparel" means "an outer garment." It has the connotation of an outer garment being worn down.

This was written primarily because of the goddess Diana who wore her dress girded up high around her loins because she was a huntress. It was the fashion of the day for women to wear their dresses that way, imitating Diana.

Paul said for them to stop dressing like the goddess Diana. We do not have Diana today, but we do have a few others.

The Bible does not say for women to walk around in sackcloth and ashes, but it does say for women to dress in orderly fashion, in reverence and with discretion.

Ladies, when you pick out clothes, keep in mind that if you purposefully buy things you know will cause men to do the double take, then you are doing it wrong. I am not saying, and neither is the Bible, that you must look like a drab old dish mop.

Christian woman in particular need to dress with discretion. You need to think about whom you are representing—whose child you are. You need to think about the fact that you are the glory of your husband.

...not with broided hair... The word "broided" means "plaited." People have said that means women are not supposed to put hair coloring on their hair, nor do anything else to make it look nice. That was not what he was talking about.

The single Greek women in the area to which Paul wrote this letter had to sit in honor of the goddess Aphrodite before they could marry. A single woman would sit in the temple with a plaitied rope about her head. She would wear a long dress, pulled tightly across her legs. Sitting in the temple, she waited until a man (whom she did not know) would come into the temple.

The man would take a coin and flip it upon her dress. She would get up, go out of the temple, and go to bed with him—thereby fulfilling her obligations to the goddess.

From that day forward, to prove that she had fulfilled her obligation, she would wear a braided or plaited cap on her head.

What about gold and pearls and costly array? The word "gold" means "golden ornaments," such as the type that were used in magic. The women of that area were great believers in the power of the evil eye.

They wore great golden necklaces used in magic and witchcraft to ward off evil spirits. The women of that day were so caught up in wearing all of this costly array that there are many accounts of women literally encasing themselves in golden bracelets from head to toe.

You can see why God would be against that. Also, they put pearls in small leather pouches and wore them to ward off evil spirits.

Paul is not saying that women cannot wear nice rings or pretty clothes. He said, do not wear things that are associated with witchcraft, or that you believe will bring you good luck.

They were so entrenched in witchcraft that they would pin gold charms on their babies' clothing. If someone came up and paid unusual attention to their child, they would try to distract their attention from the child to the gold ornament. They believed that if that person began to covet their child, the gods would take the baby away and give him to that person.

They were ignorant. They did not know the truth. Many times they would starve their children so the gods would not think that they cared about it and take it away form them. They would dress their boy child like a girl and starve him so the gods would think they didn't care much about that child, and maybe the gods would leave them alone.

11 Let the woman learn in silence with all subjection. (1st Timothy 2:11)

This is in reference to a husband and wife. It seems, upon first reading it, that women are supposed to be quiet all the time and not say anything. Stop and think, and do some studying. Let's learn what Paul meant.

The first statement, *"Let the woman learn..."* is absolutely amazing, because Paul said the women were to be allowed to learn. That statement was completely contrary to all the thinking up until that time.

In those days, women were kept ignorant. In fact, in one of the writings of the day, a leader said that for a woman to have knowledge was a curse and an evil.

When Paul made the statement *"Let the woman learn..."* it was revolutionary. He said let them learn in silence with all subjection. That word "subjection" is an interesting word in the Greek language. This is the only place where that particular word is found in the New Testament. It is not clear in the Greek text whether the word means the student is in subjection to the teacher, or the teacher is in subjection to the student. Therefore, it should be read both ways.

First of all, we need to understand that the women of that day were all ignorant. They were never allowed to be educated, never allowed to be taught, never allowed to do anything but stay in the house and have children. That was their existence.

That was not God's plan. That was the way men did it. Men set it up like that.

Paul said, *Let the woman learn in silence with all subjection.* This verse is telling us about two relationships. First, he is saying to the women, "Look, you don't know anything. We are not putting you down for it, but you have never been taught. So now, when you start being taught, be quiet. Listen to what the teacher is saying. Don't argue and contradict the teacher. Learn in quietness."

Then on the other hand, because of the meaning of the word subjection, it can also bring out the thought of Paul telling the teacher, "When you are teaching the women, don't get angry and frustrated. Don't scream and yell at them because they do not know anything. Be quiet with them. Be patient with them."

He was not saying that women could not say anything. All you have to do is turn to First Corinthians, chapters twelve, thirteen, and fourteen. This was written by the same man. He said women could prophesy, they could pray, they could do everything.

Throughout the book of Acts, and in all the epistles of Paul, Paul constantly speaks about women being preachers, women being elders, and deacons, and bishops. In Acts there are women called apostles.

How could a woman be silent and be an apostle called to preach? Why is it we believe some things?

The reason is that we take one verse of scripture and make it say what we want it to say.

For years men have wanted to dominate women—ever since Genesis 3:16.

16 Unto the woman he said, I will greatly multiply thy sorrow and thy conception; in sorrow thou shalt bring forth children; and thy desire shall be to thy husband, and he shall rule over thee. (Genesis 3:16)

12 But I suffer not a woman to teach, nor to usurp authority over the man, but to be in silence. (Or dwell in quietness.) (1st Timothy 2:12)

That word "but" in the Greek text means "by no means." That is very strong. By no means is a woman to teach nor to usurp authority over the man. That word "woman" should have been translated "wife" and the word "man" should have been translated "husband." He is saying, by no means do I allow a wife to teach nor usurp authority over her husband. The word "usurp authority" literally means "to use her self arms to get her own way."

The words "usurp authority" and "teach" work hand in hand in the thought that Paul brings out about women doing something to get their own way.

There are two words in the Greek language translated "teach." One of them literally means "to discuss things or to discuss a discourse." That is the word you find in the New Testament, when the Bible says that Jesus taught the multitudes. Paul taught in the synagogue, Philip taught in Samaria, Peter taught in Cornelius' house. That particular word means "to stand up and hold a discourse."

That is not the word found in Second Timothy 2:12. Paul is not saying that women cannot teach in the church. He is saying a woman should not use her self-arms to teach her husband a lesson or to get her own way. What are the self-arms that a wife has that she can use to teach her husband a lesson or to get her own way? It can be only one thing, since most women are not physically stronger than their husbands. It is her power of sexual persuasion. He is saying, "Wives, do not ever use your means of sexual persuasion as a tool to teach your husband something." "I'm going to teach that rascal not to do that again. I'm going to cut him off."

You may be surprised to see that the Bible talks about things like this, but it does. God is not embarrassed to talk about sex. He thought it up. It was His idea. Thank God for a God who thinks.

Do you see what Paul is saying? Do you understand that? He is saying for women not to do that. That is a good way to get your marriage in trouble.

We are spending time on the woman's role because there has been so much confusion in this area. I believe the equal rights movement has come about because of the church's failure to teach the whole counsel of God in these areas.

I am not against equal rights, and neither is God. God has never been against equal rights. If, in the last two hundred years, the church had preached what the Bible has said concerning the role and the relationship and the purpose and the plans of women, there would not be an equal rights movement in the United States today. We would not need it.

> *14 I will therefore that the younger women marry, bear children, guide the house, give none occasion to the adversary to speak reproachfully.* (1st Timothy 5:14)

"Reproachfully" means "to speak slander." He said he desires that the younger women marry, they bear children, they guide the house.

The word "guide" means "to be an instructor." In fact the word is very strong in the Greek text. It literally means "to be a ruler." This is interesting in light of the third chapter where Paul was talking to Timothy concerning the qualifications of a bishop. In First Timothy 3:4 he said a bishop was one who ruled his own house and ruled it will.

In First Timothy, chapter three, Paul said for the husband to rule his house, and in the fifth chapter he says for the wife to rule the house.

Who is to rule the house?

It seems Paul has set wives and husbands on a collision course.

No. He has set us on a course of oneness.

He is saying that the husband and wife are to share equal responsibilities in the ruling of the house. The word "guide" in the third chapter means "rule,", but it has another meaning, "to manage."

When you find a husband who is a good manager, you will find a husband who knows how to delegate authority and responsibility. He does not try to carry the whole deal on his back. It is too big. There is to much going on.

I learned a long time ago that there are certain things which my wife can do better than I. I willingly let her take care of those things. I have not lost any of my masculinity or my authority. That is just smart. The one place where you should not have to fight for self-identity is in your marriage.

1 But speak thou the things of sound doctrine:
2 That the aged men be sober, grave, temperate, sound in faith, in charity, in patience. (Titus 2:1-2)

That does not mean old men. That means the elders. A man can be an elder without being old. An elder is one who has gained and grown in wisdom and counsel. Just being old does not necessarily give you wisdom and counsel in the Word of God.

He said, let the elders be sober, grave, temperate, sound in faith, in charity, and in patience.

3 The aged women likewise, that they be in behaviour as becometh holiness, not false accusers, not given to much wine, teachers of good things. (Titus 2:3)

Can women be elders? That is what verse three says.

What are women supposed to be? Teachers of good things.

That they may teach the young women to be sober (that means wise), *to love their husbands....* (Titus 2:4)

Who would have ever thought of one woman teaching another woman how to love her husband? Love is just supposed to happen, isn't it?

No!

Good marriages do not just happen. They are the result of hard work! You find a woman who has been married to the same man for 40 years, kept him totally satisfied and happy, and she will have something to tell you. These women have something to share, something to teach.

...to love their children. (titus 2:4b)

Do you know there are many women who do not love their children? They consider them as a curse. I have heard women say, "My kids just cramp my style. I can't wait unto they are old enough to go to school, so I can go out and have fun."

5 To be discreet, chaste, keepers at home, good, obedient to their own husbands, that the word of God be not blasphemed. (Titus 2:5)

He tells them *to be discreet...* The word "discreet" means "to be self-controlled, to reign in and curb emotions and sensitive nature."

It says younger women and older women should be self-controlled. They should reign in and curb their emotions and sensitive nature.

A key to happiness and leadership is to stop walking around with your feelings extended out all over your body. Stop getting upset over little things.

Ladies, you need to understand that some of the things that mean a great deal to you do not mean that much to your husbands. That does not mean he doesn't care about you or love you. It merely means that it does not matter to him. He has a different makeup.

There are some things he is interested in that you think are dumb, and you have probably told him so. Ladies, you need to curb your sensitive nature—quit being so easily hurt and touchy.

5 ...keepers at home....

"Keepers at home" literally means "stayers at home." That does not mean you are bound to your house for the next forty years as punishment. It just means that women need to spend time at home.

5 ...good, obedient (or submissive) *to their own husbands, that the word of God be not blasphemed.* (Titus 2:5b)

The word "obedient" or "submissive" in the Greek text carries strong, strong sexual connotation. Paul is telling the women of that day—wives—to be submitted to only your own husbands sexually.

The Gentile women of that time were not used to that, and a lot of them did not like it. Paul was imploring them and commanding them to be submissive unto their husbands from a sexual standpoint.

We could look at many other scriptures along these lines, but I believe was have proven the points we set out to prove.

God can and will use women in leadership capacities. He is not against women being leaders any more than He is against men being leaders.

A woman's ability to be a leader is limited only by her ability to lead. Women can teach in the church and hold positions of responsibility in the church and community.

God's promise that you shall be the head and not the tail, above only, and not beneath, is the same to women as it is to men.

Chapter XII

SEEDS OF LEADERSHIP

Jesus revealed to us in Mark 4:26-29 that the Kingdom of God operates on the Seedtime and Harvest Law. What we put into our hearts will come out in our lives. For that reason, it is very important that we purposely plant good seed in our lives so we may harvest good fruit. This principle is true in every area of life—spirit, soul, body, financial, and social.

I recommend that you read and confess the following Seeds of Leadership about yourself on a regular basis, preferably every day. At the end of the confessions I have written some statements about what a leader is, and does, and does not do. Use them as a checklist for your own life.

Read these regularly and see how you compare. They will encourage you, instruct you, and at times, discipline you.

Remember, through the power of God's Word in your life **YOU CAN HAVE WHAT IT TAKES!**

I AM A LEADER BECAUSE...

I am more than a conqueror - Romans 8:37

I am a world overcomer - First John 5:4

I am the head and not the tail - Deuteronomy 28:13

I am above only and not beneath - Deuteronomy 28:13

I am a king and a priest - Revelation 1:6

I am reigning in life through Christ Jesus - Romans 5:17

I am free from fear - Second Timothy 1:7

I am courageous - Joshua 1:7

I am strong in the Lord and in the power of His might - Ephesians 6:10

I am seated in heavenly places in Christ Jesus - Ephesians 2:6

I am faithful - Proverbs 28:20

I am a doer of God's Word - James 1:25

I am a giver - Luke 6:38

I am a member of the body of Christ - First Corinthians 12:27

I am running to obtain the prize - First Corinthians 9:24-25

I am the salt of the earth - Matthew 5:13

I am the light of the world - Matthew 5:14

I am filled with God's Spirit - Acts 1:8

I am willing and obedient - Isaiah 1:19

God is for me - Romans 8:31

Greater is He that is in me than he that is in the world - First John 4:4

I can do all things through Christ Jesus Who strengthens me - Philippians 4:13

God has given me the victory - First John 5:4

God is my source of supply - Philippians 4:19; Psalms 23:1

I walk in love - Ephesians 5:1-2

God always causes me to triumph - First Corinthians 15:57

I have authority over Satan - Mark 16:16-18; Luke 10:19

I walk by faith - Second Corinthians 5:7

I meditate in God's Word day and night - Joshua 1:8

I have put my trust in the Lord - Proverbs 28:25

I delight in the Lord - Psalms 37:4

Jesus is my wisdom - First Corinthians 1:30

LEADERS...

are fearless in the face of adversity.

will not compromise what they know is the truth.

are slow to speak, slow to wrath, and quick to forgive.

have a disciplined prayer life.

remember where they came from.

are givers. You cannot be selfish and be a leader. A selfish leader is a tyrant.

think about what can be, not what might have been.

inspire peace and courage in others by their actions.

do not take compliments nor themselves too seriously.

know who their source is—God.

have a vision and share it with others.

are not a source of strife and division.

are meek. (i.e. Moses)

love people and look beyond their shortcomings.

have their priorities in line—God, mate, family, church, job, friends, hobbies.

major on the majors and minor on the minors. They keep things in the proper perspective.

are accountable for their actions.

are self-confident.

know what they are talking about, and are able to impart that knowledge.

lives are examples to the people who follow them.

Seeds Of Leadership

take care of themselves physically.

are willing to pay the price to accomplish their goals.

give credit to whom credit is due.

treat people with respect.

do not vacillate. They make decisions.

assume the responsibility for their actions.

do more than they are paid for.

are organized.

have initiative. They do that which ought to be done **without being told** to do it.

have a servant's heart.

do not allow the habit of procrastination to get a foothold in their lives.

protect their visions and dreams, because they are the blueprints of their ultimate success.

cannot be hurt by lies, because such attempts merely draw attention to their abilities.

make cooperation one of the most important words in their vocabulary, because without it they will fail.

see obstacles as opportunities to reach new heights, not as opportunities to fail.

are not afraid of growth in themselves and in others.

do not apologize for attempting to do something and failing. They would apologize for not trying.

Notes:

This space is provided for you to write down your own "Leadership Nuggets."

Notes

Notes

Notes

Billy Graham Crusade — God is
Bill ~~Gatt~~ Gaither **Notes** undefeated
Vocal Band — The winning
~~Cincinnati Ohio~~ —12-05-02 team
music
Channel 2 ~~Thursday~~-group Ps. 37:4 Sha
WKAR of
Cincinnati Ohio Singers Rom. 10, 11, 12 Ale
and

The Wonder of Christmas CD

Billy Graham   a living Christ

PO Box 779
Minneapolis MN.
55440

Luke 15 — The Prodigal Son — spiritual ps.
truth
you serve me with your lips — parable
but your heart is far from me.
repent — change — turn around
I Peter 2 — by His ~~stripes we~~ are ~~~~ healed

"Only one life, 'twill soon be past,
Only what's done for Christ will last"

We should not do anything we would not
want to be doing when Jesus comes, and
not go any ~~one~~ place where we would
not want to be found when He returns.